<u>Mental Armor: It's Enough</u>
<u>By C.G.Levey</u>

Mental Armor is built by the conscious choices we make to keep ourselves alive.

For ages 18 and older.

Dedicated to ALL who struggle with mental illness and those whom wish to build STRONG Mental Armor.

Survivors are already strong, but I hope to give you more strength as I call myself a survivor.

This book is to be used as a tool: It takes you through my personal experiences as case studies as well as giving you some other references to help you realize that Mental Illness requires the formation of **Mental Armor** in order to heal. Your trauma does not need to feed your mental illness in a negative way; instead, it can feed your Mental Armor and make you stronger, help you to realize when someone disrespects you, and help you learn from your past in order to be more present and less afraid of the future.

Let me be clear, I am not a professional. I am a regular person who is planning to go back to school to be a clinical social worker. Talk therapy has been helpful not only for my own mind but countless others. My need to help others with their mental illness is because of my journey in life. Mental illness to me is like a broken bone--only my **mind** is what's broken. It's painful. It hurts, only there is no X-ray to see the broken bone in my mind. You cannot see mental illness on a film and the clinical definition is changes in emotions, behaviors, and thinking that may cause distress in your everyday life. Whether that be work, home, or personal life components, our mental state has an effect on our lively activities.

Mental armor is what I came up with as a definition to describe the tools and coping mechanisms I created for myself. The choices that I clearly make to help better my life. When triggered in everyday

2

life, instead of reacting, a shield or piece of armor appears in my mind and blocks me from harm. It can be a red flashing light that states I am in danger. Some may call it the fight or flight response, only for someone who has been though as much trauma as I, triggers and warnings can escalate quickly. Mental armor is the mechanism that realizes my mind is in danger of reacting irrationally instead of responding with rational calm reasoning and smarts. Mental armor is using my brain to smartly navigate challenges and possibly harmful interactions without harming my mental state. It is clarity and a calm response to every interaction. It is making choices from a place of experience and having the self awareness to know why I am making the choice.

You are not alone.
Don't you wish ten years ago you had the information you have right now? You can be your own hero; you just have to be willing to take a good hard look at all the things you never wanted to see. Years after I wished, or even realized I needed a hero, it truly entered my head that no one else is going to save you but you. However, I didn't even think I was capable to be my own hero.

This book comes from wanting to make a difference, and to help others who are just as lost as I have been--people who have experienced trauma. I am not a professional. I am a normal human who has experienced plenty of what life has to offer. I have followed my dreams and come up short. Now I am trying to explore new avenues and I came up with an idea for an app but really I have found I just want others to find their happiness in a similar way that I have found mine. My idea for an app was called COACH. It was a clear idea to try to help others find their purpose and provide guidance but getting it going and finding the money to back the idea was large and daunting. It seemed impossible. Sitting down to write it out, my ideas and vision of what has helped me and what I have found that could help others, came quite easy. This is a book to show you as the reader my experience and how I found that I am a Happist, Kindist, and a Respectist. It is how I came to the conclusion to go back to school to get a license to help others.

Happism: the ideology of a person's innate right to find/search for what makes them happy.

Respectism: the ideology of accepting that not everyone wants what you want and having the courage to ask others questions, and the ability to understand the differences between people.

Kindism: the ideology of realizing the differences among the commonalities among all humans and not berating or disrespecting their differences. Looking at them with strength and with an inquisitive mind. Kind refers to human kind or commonality. Being kind is respecting those commonalities and not being negative about differences.

I came to these ideologies after the most profound realization. If my mother had not committed suicide, I would have tried to kill myself. Not just once but many times throughout my life. The trauma of my mother catapulted me on the path to want to help others. At first I thought this was through theater because theater was the first thing that ever helped me to feel happy. Now as I have experienced more of what life has to offer, I realize my need to help others is deep-rooted, and while theater was one outlet, one tool, I can take more of an in-depth and active role to help others one-on-one by gaining a certification through school.

Socially speaking, I can remember from a very young age being told to treat others the way I want to be treated, but this concept is wrong and disrespectful to the differences we innately have as humans. It deceives a person and specifically children from understanding that not everyone has the same views, culture, values, and definitions for everyday social, political, economic, or life backgrounds. The fact is I have found people have differing definitions for many different concepts, words, and ideologies. Even children have differing backgrounds of culture and what is acceptable in any given circumstance. We would serve our children the greatest education by teaching them to ask questions and then respecting the answers. By teaching our children about the gravity of their choices, and the responsibility of making mistakes. This can be accomplished by providing choices from very early on. If parents place more emphasis on choices earlier in life, then the positive effects on the child will be present as the kid ages and enters adulthood, and then are inundated with choices.

There is an example that I can give, and it's about the definition of a clean wash cloth. Some may define a clean wash cloth as a wash cloth they have used a few times. It doesn't smell and they haven't used it for anything that you can see visible evidence of with the naked eye. The cloth smells clean and therefore is clean. Others would say a wash cloth is only truly clean when it has been used for nothing and comes straight out of the washer/dryer. Others may be able to come up with 100 other definitions, therefore, when asking someone if they want a clean wash cloth, if I don't ask them what their definition of clean is first, then I can't properly and respectfully meet their needs. Without understanding that this person may have differing views, I cannot properly give them a choice.

Treating someone how **they** want to be treated— now that is an amazing concept. It is the first step in understanding your basic human rights to be respected and respect others. In order to do this though, you have to have the courage and understanding of your own mind to admit you cannot make decisions or choices for someone else, unless you already have been given permission. The only time this is not the case is with children. Children and young adults may not see the true consequences of their choices. They need help and guidance to set them up for the most success and to give them a good foundation for the moral and ethical choices they will face for the rest of their life.

Not having any children myself, you may say I am not qualified to speak on this subject, but I would ask you to take note that I was a child once, which gives me just as much right to talk about learning respect. Growing up, I was disrespected throughout my life leading to mental anguish and increased mental illness. Although I do not have children I have worked with children, I have nine nieces and nephews whom I have good relationships with, and I consider myself very good at observing children's needs. Oftentimes when parents have reacted to my observations by telling me "I don't have kids therefore I don't know" it is because I may have triggered an inadequacy in them by giving unwanted criticism or advice. Every time I did this, I was only ever trying to help, but I see now more than ever how I was disrespectful in my approach. I didn't ask the question of whether the person wanted my advice, or could handle it on their own.

Mental illness comes from negative stigmas and traumatic events and can be chemical. For a very long time I was ashamed to admit I had mental illness because mental illness contributed to my mother's death and it scared me to feel sick, broken, and unworthy of life's happiness. This catapulted me into sexual abuse, decreased emotional capabilities, and ultimately led to my thoughts of suicide. From now on, I will refer to mental illness in conjunction with **Mental Armor**. It is my positive spin on the life I have so far lived struggling and beating back my own mental illness, and it has provided me the strength to keep going and keep living. I am proud of my Mental Armor and saying that makes me proud to overcome my mental illness and to continue important work on myself. Everyone, for as long as they are alive, are learning creatures. Our consciousness is ever evolving and changing. The fascination I have with the human mind has always been inspiring.

1. <u>INSPIRATION</u>

Elevation is what is needed to sit down and write a book about yourself—about what you feel is judgment for your own insignificant life. You think to yourself, "I am no one, who would want to read a book about me? What makes me worthy of someone else's admiration? If I'm lucky, time is gifted to me, and someone reads my words in the least amount of effort and dismissal is the expectation at its worst?" Then the positivity comes in and says, "WHY THE FUCK NOT?"

I am approaching my thirtieth birthday, and for most of my life I have gone after what I want and done the things that I fear most. Sitting down on my bed in NYC with four roommates and a cat I love so much, I am feeling empowered and creative. In the current world we are in, having just entered 2020, I have to ask myself: How can I make the world better? My life has been privileged in ways that others haven't and I'm sure it will continue to be, but this is my attempt at creating change. I was presented with better options than others—better choices. However, everyone has the capability of bettering themselves, of helping themselves, and I did just that, with a little help from others along the way. This is my attempt at making my voice heard. I want to talk about my struggles and put my own thoughts out there to show the courage it takes, and to show others they aren't alone. To show others they too can be their own hero and fight for their life. For years I have written in journals about how I feel; I know others do the same. Now I want to put it in ink and publish my thoughts, so others can read it and see that I am no one, just like them and they can make a choice to be heard.

The inspiration of this book is my story, how I became a person I love and respect, but also it is partly inspired by blog posts I wrote when I became a Flight Attendant, writings I have done when I entered into the BDSM/Kink community, and writings of my past. Even while writing this introduction I am reminded of this post from my blog…

Lipstick, am I Feminist or Conformist?

Red, Brown, Pink, Rose, Purple. There are so many different colors I could choose to make my lips on my face stand out. The few I put above are simply the colors I tried to stick to when picking out my lipstick last night.

In two months I will start flight attendant training and then hopefully I will start flying. In every article or picture I see, the women are wearing lipstick. Ok, not every picture but a lot of them. I have to admit I feel pressured to conform and follow the crowd and paint my mouth in color to make it stand out from the rest of my features.

Here's the thing: I feel like I am cheating. Cheating on my core feminism.

I have always been a person that doesn't do things because they are cool. Generally speaking, I only partake in a fad or something the crowd is partaking in if I truly have a want for the action to occur, so by conforming to what others do, I, in a sense, feel like I am giving into what society deems I am supposed to do. In this case that is wearing lipstick.

There is another side to this debacle. I have read blogs or articles that state the importance of keeping your lips hydrated and how lipstick helps keep you looking fresh. Mainly it helps make your teeth look whiter and give your lips a pop so you can be seen rows away if an emergency happens. I certainly know that after being on an airplane for 10 hours, when I am not working I look a mess. Come time for me to work, I will need all the help I can get.

Truth is, I have always wanted to be able to wear lipstick and do it like a pro. I never understood how women, of all different walks of life, could stand having lipstick on for more than a half hour.

Last night my first stop was a MAC store in time square. I picked up a prime and prep for lips and a red lip liner. Then I went to Sephora. I had a hard time not buying everything there but limited myself to 4 more colors. A Michael Kors, Clinique, two Sephora stains, one NARS shade and two more lip liners. To say I'd over done it is probably an understatement. I came home ate dinner and could not wait to try my first combination.

Up first was the Mac lip liner and the Michael Kors Shade. Once I put everything on I was surprised how easy it was and how good it felt. I could see myself applying this regimen in a bathroom at the airport in time for me to board my first flight.

On a slightly more annoying note, this lipstick did seem to travel. It got on my hands and I am not sure how much longevity it holds but I wore it for a good 3 hours and if I hadn't gotten hungry I could have worn it for longer.

I am excited to try out each of the shades I bought. For now, I must say my feminism self feels present as long as I wear my lipstick as a shield of pride and not out of obligation.

■■■

Little did I know at the time of writing this that lipstick would be a driving force in later me not working for that airline anymore. It would be a catalyst to a great deal of hurt and pain because wearing lipstick as a woman should be a choice and not something forced upon you because of gender.

I believe in creativity and I believe in sharing yourself in order to give others the opportunity and courage to share themselves. This is healing but also everything in this is from my point of view— my personal point of view and not from a professional standpoint.

This is an account of no one special except to those I hold dear and a simple recount of my own womanhood and growth to being a healthy adult which is a struggle each and every day.

Dedicated to everyone trying to become their own person, and for those looking for the strength to be their own hero.

Feminist: A person who believes in equal rights to choice no matter your gender specifically as it pertains to those identifying as female, but only because I identify as female. A man or someone who identifies as other genders can also be a feminist.

Conformist: A person who acts or makes a choice out of obligation because of pressures from familial, social, political, or other outside influencing factors, having a lack of individual or personal motivation. Lack of agency in making a choice that may feel discriminatory based on a person's individual ideals of human rights.

After watching a few documentaries and plenty of interviews about people I often think to myself about what makes them special; everyone has a story; everyone has had bad things happen to them. The Corona Virus of 2019 hit during my waiting time period, and I had to go back and add to this book to express the widely different world we are now coming to experience. The question I want to answer is: **What is it that separates those that have the platform to share how they have acquired this ability to endure trauma and build their Mental Armor to turn mental illness into a positive driving force?**

It's the courage to decide to share their story. In the past few years a lot of feminist movements have come out, including #Metoo and #Timeisup. We have seen the popularity of RBG come into prominence as she categorically fights for equality and serves as a role model for feminism. RBG is effective because she fights not just for women, but humans. She is an OG human rights activist. She fights and I fight for RESPECT. I want to re-define this word and make sure it can be more easily understood in terms of others, but more importantly in terms of our self respect.

On a YouTube video about Emma Watson, it was described in the video that she suffers from **Imposter Syndrome and a lightning bolt went through my body.** I have that. No matter what success I have or what makes me happy I think to myself, "This is a mistake. I don't belong here. I don't deserve the good. What makes this happiness ok for me?" I feel like an imposter. I feel worthless. I don't belong. Why have I never heard of imposter syndrome before?

Emma Watson herself has used her platform and fame for immense positivity and tried to make the world a better place and one that aligns with her morals, ethics, beliefs, and view as to how others can lift one another up and be there for each other. I love her self-partnered proclamation, and adopted that myself once I felt it was a true label.

Increasingly and with great guilt, I often wake up and feel inadequate like I am no one that matters. Let me paint you the picture of my insecurity:

It is like I have a teenager that lives inside my brain. He (yes it is a he) constantly is shouting insults and disrespectful, hurtful things to me at all times, as if I am his parent and I have disrespected his needs. He is me, yelling at the adult version of myself inside my own mind. In order for me to gain more confidence and stop listening to the petulant insecure teenager who doesn't know who I am, I need to quiet him, send him to his room so he can calm down, and then once he is ready, to tell me why he was acting the way he was and being hurtful. Then it allows me to see my insecurities for what they are, which is usually fear of abandonment, or admonishment, or inexperience. It all is about fear. Any time I have ever been rude or mean or made a wrong choice knowingly, it has been because this teenage male part of me was driving my choices instead of my true self. My adult self, as I am now.

This all stems back to my mother committing suicide, but I know others feel this way no matter their life experiences—no matter their trauma. It also stems from societal pressures. I am no one and I do deserve good things, because I am living and have made the choice to live. If I don't choose to follow my heart and to try and help others realize they are not nothing, then maybe I am a waste of my own humanity. I bring myself joy; I make myself laugh; I build up those around me and those I come in contact with as much as possible. I believe in being kind and treating each person with respect. Even if it is basic respect.

The society we live in right now is divided and polarized in many different ways and people all over are trying their hardest to bring awareness to all sorts of topics, whether it be climate change or sexism or political issues. These topics affect the world around us and our own beliefs and perspectives. They affect our humanity which lives within our mind. My biggest goal is to express that there are normal yet idyllically weird people out there that continue the day to day grind to make other people's lives better by simply being themselves. Mental Illness is only as powerful as what each individual decides in terms of power. There is no other way to show this with integrity than to first share my own story in full, with as much detail as I deem respectful to those it involves.

The more I write about my inspiration and what lead me to where I am now the more I realize who I am now is largely due to a multitude of factors. Let's list just a few contributing factors that will be further explored in chapters but just to kick off the type of content to expect:

Family: The people I consider my family have been a huge factor in who I am as a person. My parents and siblings gave me my morals; friends and family, whom I trust now, help me with their opinions and experiences to potentially help guide my choices. Family has been a huge positive force in my life but it has also brought some of the biggest heartbreak and most of my major triggering events from childhood. However, I would not be the happy healthy human I am today without them. They are both positives and negatives in my life. I make the choice to look at them positively, and not blame them for the negatives. Part of respect is understanding that they did the best that they could with the knowledge they had. People cannot be responsible for the things they do not know. This is why education is extremely important. Education can be in the form of family, school, or life experience.

Work: Going to school as a kid work was described as my job, I had a few jobs in high school and then in college I started working in theater. I continued doing so throughout that last 10 years professionally. Recently I realized I really want to do talk therapy and have taken steps to get a formal education to do so as a clinical social worker. My ultimate goal is to provide talk therapy, and I also write creatively. Creating is one of my many joys in life, and always has been.

Society: Although I wish this wasn't a factor in who I am, social standards are a part of the mix. We all are taught from an early age what is and isn't acceptable socially by the world we live in. That world, as we are learning in 2020, can change drastically and make us feel trapped. Unfortunately, when we are first taught, the way we see the world is greatly influenced by those that teach us. This can be in the form of actual teachers or content we read or the arts and entertainment. While traveling through life, until our brains stop forming; we understand the power we have in forming our own opinions, we rely on our foundations that get built in the earliest years of living. These foundations come from those who take care of us from 0-5, and then from their more people start to influence our reality.

Sex: We live in a world that is obsessed with sex. Even people that believe sex is wrong or only meant to be for reproduction purposes are obsessed with it. There is a quote from The Newsroom written by Aaron Sorkin: "The world is split into two types of people, those that love sex and those that are utterly repulsed by it. I happen to be one of the people that love sex." This statement is the epitome of sex for me in terms of concept. The good stuff you will just have to keep reading to find out how good it will get in terms of sexual exploration. What I can tell you is it took a very long time to admit my sexual abuse from the past. Exploring sex was insurmountably helpful in healing the physical and mental wounds that I sustained from past abuse. My sexual Mental Armor is now strong.

In the last three years I have found I love talking to people about life—about what makes them tick—about the reasoning behind why they are the way they are exactly themselves. About the choices they make that are different than the ones I would make. I find the different roads someone can take to be inspiring in their unique turns and the choices people make are, in themselves, captivating. Differences are beautiful and I idealize them.

Now in my almost-thirties I have realized how I envision my own life as a road. I don't believe my life is predetermined, and I do not believe in a driving force other than myself and the choices I make. Some that may think god predetermines life may look at life like a maze, whereas I see it as creating my own maze. Throughout my life I have been agnostic, meaning I don't necessarily believe in a god or any deity, but I can't prove one does not exist. I look at life from a scientific and respectful way. I do however respect everyone's right to choose for themselves what's right for their lives, and if religion plays a part in your choices, I understand the questions I can ask to be respectful to others beliefs. This brings me to respect.

Respect should probably be its own chapter later. It definitely will be but if I am being true to myself it is one of the biggest inspirations in writing this book. Learning about respect happened by living with my eldest sister and her husband, and was one of the biggest educational experiences of my life. Then respect was re-enforced by a YouTube video that has been done by many different people and is meant to teach consent to kids and others:

Consent is as easy as tea is the YouTube video that goes through how to know when someone gives consent for sex, but it also deals with the basic guidelines of respect in that if someone says no, it means no. In Chapter 6 the topic of respect and consent will be further discussed.

Throughout my exploration into who I am and who I want to become, past, future and present, I have read many books to enlighten myself on all the topics I will be covering. That notion in general is interesting. Why is it that I needed to read books on self-esteem, respect, confidence, and how to relate to people? Why is it that I fear succeeding more than I fear failing? How much of my trauma from prior years really affects the person I am now? Why can't I be here and now and not over think every situation?

These questions can be haunting and I struggle with them just like any other person— whether that be a CEO or a celebrity or my best friend in the whole world or family, or a stranger I have yet to encounter.

The only thing that stops me from sharing my story is me… so here goes.

2. <u>*MILESTONES*</u>

Being born in 1990 I am definitely a millennial. I love the memes that talk about how weird my generation is because we remember a time when computers were not around and cell phones didn't exist, but those huge leaps in technology happened while we were just starting out. They have provided for an immense growth in education and knowledge. Not to mention the huge impacts that 9/11 had.

Strangely enough I remember being in the towers a year before 9/11 and to this day I resonate with the tragedy and how it changed everything. Fear was now something everyone knew. Which is interesting because I knew it all too well. Looking back, I was greatly desensitized to 9/11.

There I go, getting ahead of myself.

What does it even mean to be born a girl?

Recently, I watched a documentary talking about how much pressure is placed on gender. It is called InterSEXtion on Netflix, and it was truly enlightening. We live in a society that predominantly places each person into either female or male roles. Other societies have multiple genders; they do not rely on male or female. This is rapidly changing.

I believe everyone should have the ability to identify themselves in whatever manner they want. I have always identified as a woman. I do believe society has made it extremely difficult for anyone, who doesn't fall into the two genders, to feel accepted in society.

Personally male, female, and non-binary are the three genders, but I also believe that these labels do not need to constrict anything but the parts in which you were born. Once you become a mature person, you gain the knowledge about your personal preference to, choose to be what gender you believe yourself to be, if that is even important. Who would I be to tell you who you are? I cannot determine that. I do not have any right to name you unless I also give you the right to determine what I am, which you do not have that right.

We choose a baby's name as soon as they are born based on their gender. It is a construct that I believe we have been trained to do to make people more like that which we are familiar with. We grew up in a society that has males and females and anything different is socially too weird. However, this is disrespectful to those born different, which is in fact all of us.

As a young girl I remember feeling out of place because I didn't like dolls, except to play with their hair, and because I thought I should. I also wanted to be able to do my own hair one day. In fact, I didn't enjoy dolls at all. I loved playing with hair though and I loved playing with clothing, but not just female clothing. I remember wanting to dress more like a boy; I knew my dad wanted me to be a boy. I wanted to make him proud.

Very early on I remember feeling pressure toward certain things that now as an adult I feel were gender specific, and I don't think this was on purpose but I had two older sisters and therefore it wasn't surprising. However I also felt drawn to more boyish activities because of the pressure that I wasn't a boy.

In my early years of learning that there was a difference in gender from girls and boys, I don't remember being taught about other options. I was taught about vaginas and penises and how one belonged to a female and the other to a male. Now as an adult I know about transgender and non-binary and I still identify as female; however, as a kid there were only two options.

Being the youngest of three girls I was dressed in hand-me-downs and I had built in mentors as to what it meant to be a girl. The problem was, if I didn't want to make those choices, how was I supposed to not follow the examples of my sisters? This was what was expected of me?

I did not particularly relate to my sisters. I wanted to not be treated as a gentle little girl. I remember wanting to be different then my sisters. I wanted to be a boy. Growing up I was told how much my dad wanted a boy. I thought it was disappointing that I was a girl. My parents may not have understood that was the message they sent me; in fact I didn't realize until I was an adult that this was the message I heard. I do remember feeling guilty for not being the boy my dad wanted. I remember them telling me how they made the choice to have me, which was because my mom worried if something would have happened to one of my sister's they didn't want any of us to be alone. I felt like an insurance baby.

This guilt disappeared as I got older and there were other ways I made my dad proud. I spent a few years being a tomboy and playing sports to get over the guilt that was unknowingly placed on me. This wasn't his fault; he didn't realize I paid this much attention to his words.

He didn't realize that when he flirted with pretty waitresses that I was paying attention to the attention he gave them, and I wanted his attention. He didn't realize how much responsibility being an adult, a role model, a male to a female child, held gravity in life and specifically my life.

When I was very little I did gymnastics. It was something I remember being very passionate about. I loved countless things about flipping through the air and I loved the power I felt in the gym. I loved the femininity of it. I felt graceful and cute. It made me proud to be a gymnast.

My parents decided to not pursue gymnastics at a time when I wasn't allowed to make my own choices in the matter. I didn't know why the decision to not do gymnastics was made. They told me it was about money, but I thought it was about being a girl. There is a part of me that is thankful because who knows what heights I could have gone to, and in a way with everything that happened with USA Gymnastics, it's possible that decision was a savior for me.

Soccer later became my sport and a huge help in the guilt I felt over not being the boy my father wanted me to be. I remember him claiming the pride he had for the kind of athlete I was and I realized, possibly for the first time, that I had more choice in my future than I thought. I could be a girl and still do things boys could do. To this day, I can't tell you if I knew this at the time of feeling this type of realization. Looking back that is how I remember the change, but it took me a very long time to even admit I wanted to be a boy at one point. It took even longer to admit I was happy that I never tried to transition to be one.

Being a girl, I found it incredibly difficult. My childhood feels like it ended early and before it even started and therefore anytime something bad happened I thought it was just what it was: it was normal, it was expected. The pain I felt was routine.

When is it exactly that you go from being a child, to a little kid, to no longer being a child, then to teen years which also have gender roles, to being a young adult, to being a full adult? Who determines these rights of passage?

Infant = 0 – 3: Total reliance on adults for all needs

Child = 3 – 11: Starts to form more cognitive personality and eventually can reason, prime years to gain morals and habits for communication (11 is flexible as the cap on Childhood. Gaining maturity in a more innocent fashion only applies if nothing traumatic happens forcing a kid to grow up faster… * If a traumatic event happens it can catapult a kid to adult or possibly if not raised in an environment that has love and consistency this can trigger more adult thoughts.)

Teen = 12 – 19: These years are the building blocks to adulthood and being autonomous. This is largely due to education and schooling. If proper communication has been taught up until this point then when conflict comes up, hopefully a teen already has the tools to be a contributing member to the solution and can express themselves enough to be able to show the adults the teen relies on that they have the ability to keep making the safe and responsible choices.

Adult: 19 – death: Making all life choices and understanding the full effects of those choices. Making the choice every single day to keep going no matter how much success or failure you endure, understanding that life keeps going on three conditions:

1. You make the choice every day to keep living.
2. Everything is not in your control (Shit happens).
3. Your choices are the only thing you have so choose wisely.

The transition into being an adult can happen at any time in my opinion. Just because you are an adult does not mean you are well adjusted, or healthy, or whole, or any other descriptive word. It's autonomy in choosing how you want to live.

Healthy Adult: When you work to make your life, yourself, and those around you brighter and happier, and work every day to live life how you want to live it. Making choices that first

adhere to your self-respect and the
priorities that you hold, and then
adhering to the respect you hold for
others.

In aviation one of the best lessons I learned
was a way to describe respect. When a
decompression happens, we are taught that those 3-
5 seconds, depending on altitude, matter in terms of
saving your life. If you pass out, then you cannot
help anyone else. I approach my mental illness in
the same way. I need that mask, as my armor, and I
need to save myself before I save others.

My childhood was cut short by trauma, and I
quickly embodied my definition of being an adult. I
recently realized in therapy that I cannot remember
ever feeling taken care of, or cared for by adults in
my life, even though I know they did take care of
me. As a kid I had a roof over my head, I was never
starving, and know that I was privileged. Yet I don't
remember what it was to feel safe growing up. I
didn't even know what feeling safe was until I was
in my late 20's. I didn't even know I didn't feel safe
growing up until I was 29. No one ever described or
asked me if I felt safe, and I didn't know I had a
right to feel safe.

**Family and society failed me in giving me
the tools**, that now as an adult I have, but only
because I worked my ass off to get them. I love my
parents, and thank them for all that they did, but I
also must thank myself for the work I did as a child

and check in with myself each step I take. Don't misunderstand: my parents, and specifically my step-mom did their best, and I would not be who I am now without them. I have immense respect for my parents. It's possible they meant to give me some of the information I now rely on as an adult, but maybe they didn't know how to tell me, or they tried to but missed the mark. They did their best.

How I wish that the theories and information had been given to me earlier in life so that I could have never thought that I was wrong, or defective, or inadequate, or worthless. I wish I could have felt more confident sooner, and yet part of my self respect and self love is accepting my own journey to these realizations that I want to share. How I wish that someone would have asked me how I feel about myself. Had they asked what my interactions in this world meant at the time I was confused by them. Had they asked how we as humans attribute emotion to each experience, and most important, how to communicate in the ways needed to be healthy.

These are the main driving forces for each work I write. Whenever I write I do it with the hope that it may bring me closer to others and allow them to know they are not alone. That it may allow them to pick apart the teachings I have gathered and know that I and everyone are just trying to figure life out one milestone at a time. That, however weird they may be, they find peace and hope and joy in being weird.

3. TRAGEDY

We all have guilty pleasures. One of mine is to watch The Bachelor. I love watching that show from an anthropological standpoint. It shows life in a strange confined social experiment. Secretly I wish I was the type of woman the producers would have on that show. When I get real with myself, I think how they would never cast someone like me. I'm too honest, I can't be controlled and would say whatever I want, and the girls would love me too much. Well, the ones who understand respect would love me; those that have triggers that I aggravate would hate me. I think that they'd make me out to be the villain if I went on a show like that. **Why is it I feel like this whole paragraph is a plea to put me on the bachelor? It's not.**

The truth is, I love watching a show like that because it's good entertainment—the stories and the drama. It is great storytelling television. It's the best theatrical television and I love it. Reality TV at its worst or best depending on perspective. It also makes me feel less alone in my hardship, because it shows real life in a raw way. I think my main fascination is I would love the experience just to see what choices I would make, kind of my own anthropological experiment. I have never liked receiving attention but the idea of seeing the whole thing play out is captivating. It would bring self insight, which brings me to my sad story.

When I was five, my mother died. The red lights rotating on their axes outside my apartment are still burned into the globe on my memory reel. The four of us had gone to my grandmother's beach house for my sister's birthday celebration. My mother was supposed to meet us there. She never showed.

We drove back into the city. I remember getting out of the car and my dad had us go to friend's house across the street. Now I see he was protecting us, but I was very confused by this at the time. I remember the lights. I remember my father coming in and telling us all that our mother had died. I remember not understanding what that meant. I remember seeing everyone crying and thinking that I had to be the strong one because they were sad and I wasn't. I remember feeling responsible for making them feel better, and the empathy I had for their pain. I was scared, because I didn't know what a mom was, and I didn't know what death really was or why they were sad about it. I loved them though, and so I became very protective, and wanted to cheer them up. That's what I had been taught.

My memories after this are a bit hazy, as are my memories before. I have only a couple memories of my mother. I remember a family trip to Disney World. I remember a few dinners out at restaurants. A few birthdays. My dad re-married. We moved to South Jersey. I started growing boobs around eight. They grew fast.

Around eleven is when I started being sexually abused. I didn't know this was happening at the time. I was so desperate for attention and friends that I took attention any way I could get it. Unfortunately, around this age is when boys start wanting to be touched themselves and therefore, because they have been taught to "treat others the way you want to be treated," I started getting touched or offering to let others touch my body to make friends. I felt obligated to and didn't know my body was mine to choose what to do with. I hadn't been shown what respect was, and had no clear definition of it. Looking back, this was due to a lack of respect that I always observed adults having toward kids, or others. Sometimes I wish I had a dollar for every time I was asked the question "What size are your boobs?". Like men can even comprehend the size of boobs that don't fit into normal range of breast size.

Then I was in middle school and thirteen. My memory then started to get better at drawing the details. It was work to get the pictures to be more and more memorable and detailed. This was thanks to my step-mom. It took a family argument that resulted in my step-mom physically shaking me till I cried. She didn't harm me, her grip was soft but firm, and it worked in allowing me to feel emotions that are crucial to making choices. I cried and it was ok for her to see it, it was ok for me to show my family my emotions. For them to see.

I'm not saying that was the right or wrong or any kind of way to get the result of feeling but it worked. She wasn't hurting me; she was freeing me. I was genuinely surprised. This is when, as I'll talk about more in depth, I started to explore who I am and why I work the way I work. I was emotionally numb until this point, not allowing myself to feel things in the open, and not allowing others to get close to me because I was afraid of them choosing to abandon me in the same way my mother did. I was afraid of my own power.

At thirteen I had already been sexually assaulted more times than I could count. I had no way to communicate this because I didn't even really understand what *this* meant. Coming to terms with it while it continued to happen was hard. I was unaware of how to speak up. Who to tell? How to tell? Would I be believed? Would they blame me? What was even wrong with the interactions? What effect it had on me? How it made me feel? I only just started dealing with the sexual assaults that have happened to me earlier in life now, at almost thirty. Even now I don't truly believe it was the other kid's fault, but it doesn't change that it happened, and to the adults who abused me, it doesn't change the shame I now feel years later for never speaking up for myself.

I started developing breasts when I was eight, had full grown breasts by twelve and large pendulous breasts by thirteen to fourteen. I used to wear sports bras to be more boyish to help deter male peers from trying to touch my boobs. I had already been exposed to materials or ideas that didn't necessarily describe respect in terms of relationships or sex, or what to do when you got the attention I got, and I had not been taught that when it comes to my body. I admittedly allowed a boy to touch my breasts so I could be considered a cool kid. I didn't know why; I didn't know these things were wrong at that age. I didn't really want to do that, but didn't have enough moxie, or agency, or nerve to say NO and honestly I was not sure the boys would have taken my "No" as a NO. I can't exactly pinpoint why I never told on the kid that grabbed both boobs while I was hanging on a soccer goal post the real reason it upset me. Or spoke up that it made me uncomfortable. To this day I have no idea where my voice disappeared to when countless men thought they had rights to touch my body. I do know that I wanted to be wanted; I wanted to have friends. I wanted to be liked and respected, but I was without the tools to do this without my body at that age. I felt like a child prostitute.

I remember being warned at fifteen when visiting my older sister at college that I needed to be careful because I was a danger to men. I was jailbait. That my body didn't make me look like a fifteen-year-old and that I could ruin a man's life if

I did anything with them. That night I was told this I
made out with two boys. Two boys that were at
least four years older than me. My sister went off to
sleep with some guy and I don't specifically
remember the rest of the night. I don't think
anything happened. I think I remember going back
to her dorm and going to sleep. I remember being
upset that my sister ditched me for a guy. After all,
she deserved to have fun. Why was I as a fifteen-
year-old responsible for the actions of a man? Why
did being told that I could get a guy in trouble made
me feel more like a sexual object? Why wasn't I
being told no one had a right to touch me if I didn't
want them to?

Logically, and now, I understand that I was
told about my responsibility toward men because
we all have responsibilities to our fellow humans.
However, it doesn't change that it affected my
sexual life. I already felt responsible, and now I felt
responsible for every time a boy or man laid a hand
on me and I didn't want that responsibility. I felt
silenced because of the damage others could do to
me, and not empowered to say the harm they may
cause me. There was no regard for the damage they
could do to me. Once I became sexual four years
later, my notion of sex being a man's choice that
mattered more than my own choice compounded
the idea that I could never trust a man's intentions
because I felt like a sex object. I started having
panic attacks, at nineteen, because I felt taken
advantage of and like my agency was gone—and
there was no choice.

My worth at that time in my life was low. I
felt more alone than I ever had. I felt small and
insignificant, I felt worthless.

My mother had killed herself and from what
I had learned up to this point about what a mother's
role should be, I couldn't fathom why she would
leave me and my sisters. Why would she leave us to
be protected by people who may not be as capable
as her? I felt responsible for her death no matter
how many times someone explained her mental
illness to me. It loomed over me, like a rain cloud
ready to let out the buckets of water.

My faith in myself to speak up with my
voice to say anything and be heard was nonexistent.
I thought her killing herself was my fault. No one
had ever explained anything to me in a way that
made sense, because no one asked me the right
questions to understand how my brain worked. Why
should I speak up to have more answers not given?
Why should I speak up to be disrespected yet again?
I was a child when she died, I didn't know what
death was, I didn't know it wasn't my fault. She
was sick, I didn't know what a mother was; I didn't
know how I would later feel about her death or how
it would quite literally affect my entire life and all
my relationships.

When the funeral happened I remember that
my grandmother came in the room and asked my
sisters and I if we wanted to see mommy before

they closed the casket. At the time I remember saying yes because someone said it was the last time I'd see her, and at the time I knew enough about myself to know I needed to see her one last time. **I will always be grateful for that self awareness at that age.** We, as humans, were born to make choices and somehow I knew what I needed in that very moment. I was the only one out of my siblings that went to see my mom lying in her coffin. She was lifeless and I could tell it was no longer her, just her body. The realization that I was not enough to keep her here, fighting for life, experiencing life, haunted me until my mid 20's and no one but me helped me through that realization. Other's influenced the journey but I had to interpret the languages and story for myself. I had those that contributed, but I had to be open to them, in order to hear what they were saying to let their help sink in to my thick brain.

That got dark real quick… breaking the fourth wall for a second. Take a breath it's ok. This is ultimately a happy story. Believe me when I say there will be highs as well as maybe a couple more lows to come <3. I appreciate you reading. I cried while I wrote this.

Having a mother die at such a young age is unimaginable for most but for me, it was my reality. The occurrence, as I stated, affected my entire life thus far, but the biggest thing I remember in that moment of my father telling us of her death, is that I wanted to be strong because it was the only way I felt I could help. I wasn't sad myself because I didn't know what was really happening. How could I? I was five.

When I was seven I remember trying to make friends and it was extremely difficult. No matter what I did other kids my age didn't seem to want to be my friend. I did have a next-door neighbor that I became friends with at eight. The truth is I distanced myself from other kids because I was scared that like my mother they would abandon me. I was always afraid of the pain that came from another's choosing to disrespect me by respecting their own needs.

My first thoughts of suicide came to mind throughout middle and high school when making friends was increasingly harder because of my worries and anxieties over making friends. I would often come on too strong and scare people because I wanted them to like me. I always knew that other people cannot like you or understand you unless you show them who you are, and I was never afraid of my wants to be liked or wanted. I remember being rejected by kids at school which fed my abandonment issues, and if I was thinking about suicide because of my loneliness and pain, then others were in that same boat. Silence was too often a part of my schooling, and it felt dangerous to keep it to myself, but I didn't have anyone to share it with.

One day in eighth grade I remember being
handed a note from the people I thought were my
friends. The note is a note I still have at my parent's
house. I am not sure why I kept it as it caused me
immense pain and hurt. Probably to re-read it and
see if I had healed the wounds that were caused by
it. It read that I was annoying, that I was too intense
and that because I seemed to like the girls too much
and wanted to be their friends, they asked me to no
longer sit with them at lunch as I was creepy and
overly interested in being liked. The note was
written by the girls, and the boys didn't feel the
same. However, they had never told me I was
annoying. They had never given me the chance to
do better and they hadn't shown me the respect of
acknowledging my good intentions of wanting to be
their friend. I was crushed. This furthered my
feelings of abandonment; it caused me to further
withdraw and to think I would go through life
without friends and be always alone. My middle
sister was actually very helpful in this specific time.
As I got off the bus she drove down the street. She
noticed I was crying and consoled me. She tried to
tell me the truth, but there was no quieting the voice
inside my head that said I was worthless,
disposable, and nothing.

I remember thinking, how could I allow
myself to get close to someone that could make the
same choice my mother did and abandon me? How
could I knowingly give my heart to someone that
could leave me? Then, the same reasons that I was
afraid of making friends then caused me to be

clingy and overly enthusiastic when someone showed interest in me. It was increasingly circular. If it weren't for my family, I would not be alive today. I truly don't know how people who don't have family choose every day to stay on this earth and I give them all the positivity that I can, I try to be there for them in any way I can, and they are my true inspiration in everything I share. My purpose is trying to find people I can help with my own experiences and knowledge, mostly because I wish I had me, as I am now, in my life when I was five. My step-mom was almost there; she did her best. I have an immense amount of love and respect for my family. They did keep me alive until I could take on the full responsibility myself.

It has always come down to the fact that I love my family and I don't want to cause the same hurt my mother caused when she died. That's what my family has done; they saved and continue to save my life every day. When I talk about family I mean all of those that are in any of my circles of relations that I rely on for my happiness and support. The people with whom I relate and love are the most important thing in my life. Not all of them are my blood but I love all of them in different ways.

4. NO ONE

Speaking of relationships, let me explain the bull's-eye of relationships in my eyes. When we enter this world we have a relationship bull's eye. When you are a baby it's easy: you have one ring because your needs are simple—eat, sleep, poop, and the need for comfort or love. Eventually you start needing more stimuli. Then more ways to communicate. Basic needs have to be covered, and the workload is relatively tiring because of the limitation of babies' capabilities to communicate— but not all that difficult.

As I have aged I have found the needs and wants in life to create more circles of relationships, and at any given moment people can travel further or closer to the center circle. Just because someone crosses to an outer circle doesn't necessarily mean they are off the bulls-eye; it just means they do not get as much of your time, attention, or anything you deem important in terms of maintaining a relationship. The further out on the bulls-eye, the less effort you must put in to the relationship. However, it doesn't make it any less important to the person at the center of the apparatus.

No one is a great humble tool to use when I start to think badly about myself. Every single person starts out as No One—just a baby. Some have greater advantages than others. These advantages can be in family or personality or intelligence or money. Possibly an advantage may been seen by others as a disadvantage, like a disability or cognitive skill that is lacking. I certainly know I didn't come from nothing in terms of monetary wealth but in terms of self-capabilities, no one gets to judge where I come from but me.

Pride is pretty powerful. It can be negative or positive. I choose to look at a healthy amount of pride as very positive. In my experience, pride can be someone's downfall and it can be a strength. Believing in yourself is different than being overly confident. Is pride an equivalent to confidence?

In some ways this could be talked about in gender discrimination. I've been the woman that has been told my pride is getting the better of me, but then walked away to think, "If I was a man would that person had said the same thing?"

Our relationship with ourselves is determined by no one and yet our relationships with others are only 50% in our hands. I struggle to rely on others because at any time they could decide to leave. At any time, I may disrespect them in a way that is unforgivable to their own self respect. It is continuously hard when people tell me one thing and then their actions do the opposite. Honesty has become a lost courtesy as well as true respect and having integrity. I say courtesy because it isn't required and we are taught to lie so early on. Lying can actually be important in terms of not hurting people's feelings intentionally, but it can also be extremely disrespectful if used improperly.

I was hammered with the fact that if someone you love doesn't have the whole truth then they cannot help you when you need their help. My step-mom was a public defender. She came home often with stories about these regular people who had made choices that landed them in their situation, oftentimes in jail or prison. Looking back on it now it's apparent that even at the time of hearing those stories, in the back of my head I thought to myself, they could always kill themselves.

No one is exempt from the possibility to leave this world with no explanation and just be gone. Therefore, I had to figure out a way to push through and find joy in the relationships that were important. Including my relationship with myself.

Relationships can be anything from an acquaintance to family. Recently I had a realization about a few friends of mine. They were no longer just friends, but I consider them a part of my family. This realization was an extremely positive change from previous parts in my life, where I was convinced I was unlovable and could not be loved by anyone other than those obligated to love me.

No one knows where anyone is in their life until they get to know them at their core—their values, their experiences; we are the sum of our parts. Even then, who are you to make any determination except for yourself of someone's value? I had to understand this power before coming to terms with how I felt in prior situations in my life.

Throughout my career I had people describe this concept that you can never know someone fully and everyone is no one until they become someone, so when I come into any situation I started looking at people going into their second act. You have a first act, but any number of things could have gone right and any number of things could have gone wrong. **What is important are the choices you then choose to make with the knowledge you currently have to move forward and have the best second act you can possibly have.**

Gaining pride and being proud of my choices was not an easy thing to accomplish. Not allowing my pride to prevent me from failing is one of the driving forces behind each and every decision I make. I love failing because I have done it all my life and oftentimes, when I fail, I learn the most about me, and about others.

You miss 100% of the opportunities you don't try for and yet I worry about all the opportunities I didn't or may not take. I was watching Marvelous Mrs. Maisel the other night and it was the third season and Susie and Midge are in the casino putting pennies in a machine, saying

"That could have been something, that could have been something." They go back and forth. It just so happens I am watching this with my best friend, my soul mate. We coincidentally are going to Vegas for my thirtieth birthday and we couldn't stop laughing at the idea that we are definitely going to be doing that when we are in Vegas. Which of course then we did do.

My best friend hadn't planned on being over that night but was here in my bed being possibly the best human. No one may ever measure up to her and I hope without question I enrich her life as much as she enriches mine. I feel this way about few people in this world and the fact that she is a part of my family, is not taken for granted.

Other friends have come and gone and this one seems to have stuck as much as I hope I am sticking in her life. However, because I have had other friends I thought would forever be this close I know more than most that people move on the bull's-eye. It is a fluid apparatus that I envision to help me determine choices in my relationships. All I can do is be open to the fluid nature of each relationship and hope that the ones I want to stay stuck to, want me as much as I want them. Finding like-minded people is like spotting a unicorn.

Here is a blog post on this specifically:

People who are worth your time… finding a unicorn

Making friends is hard. Finding people to trust with your secrets and with your heart is a difficult task.

Work is not the first place I would look for friends but every so often I come across a person with whom I can see being a good friend—being a good person to me.

This makes me think about the potential I see in each person when I meet them. Most people I meet at work I see only a professional work potential. They are good at their job, and I respect them for how they do their job.

It is rare to come across someone with whom I feel I can have a work relationship and also have a friendship with. Even more so, it is rare to find someone who feels the same way and can value finding someone they can be friendly with at work to be a unique person… it's a unicorn.

It's scary to let someone in. It's the expectation and the hope that they will reciprocate, but when you find a person from your work that you want to let into your personal life, it's very much like finding a unicorn.

I'm am happy to say I have found very few in my professional career but they do exist and I am damn happy to call a colleague a friend when they earn the title/have the courage to make me their friend.

It's rare to fly in my company with someone more than a few times within a short time. I have had the pleasure of flying with some really fantastic people multiple times and when their names appear on my schedule I am truly delighted. I'm even more delighted when I can take note at how lucky I am to fly with someone in a professional environment but also be able to call that professional my friend. How lucky am I, to find unicorns where I work?

Broad City comes to mind in relation to finding people to be friends with who respect the weird nature of life. Who respect my individual weird nature. That show is an inspiration as are its writers. Ilana Glazer and Abbi Jacobson are creators I admire for their depiction of friendship. **If no one is particularly special because everyone is special, then finding those who you individually find special is unique and wonderful in itself**. Why is it that we don't show ourselves as much admiration as we show those with whom we surround ourselves? Why is it so hard to love and respect ourselves without disrespecting others?

When I did come across people who showed interest in being my friend growing up, it was very hard for me to think they were genuine in their affection for me. I was distrustful of their intentions to be my friend because of the pain and abandonment from my mother and the rejection and cruelty that was shown to me by my peers. It was hard to trust that they would accept me and love me the way I viewed those concepts. The only way that changed was with time.

6. TIME

When I started high school, little did I know how much I would grow during those four years. I had trouble making friends. Finally, after a couple of years I found friends in the theater department. They were accepting and encouraging. I decided that theater was going to be my salvation—my home. I loved everything about it.

Time is a funny thing and how there have been times in my life that have felt circular because they feel similar to another point in my life. Almost like different versions of my same self. Whenever I come across a big choice it brings me back to the last big choice I made. The advice I have received. The pros and cons. How it will affect me and those I care about. It all gets measured.

My senior year in high school my world stopped. Three major events tested me as I had never been tested before with as much cognition that I had at those moments.

1. The board of Education tried to censor the theater department and we fought them to do the musical that was chosen

for us by the director and leader of the spring musical.

2. A teacher with whom I was close put himself in a position to be falsely accused of misconduct with a student. It was later revealed the student made up the allegations and then became ashamed and eventually admitted to the entire issue having been made up. The teacher did not return to my school to teach.

3. My step-mom was hit, as a pedestrian, by a drunk driver. She came away from the accident with a broken leg and nerve damage in her arm and PTSD. However, she could have died.

These happenings tested my abilities as the adult I now realize I was, even though I was not legally an adult. I was not ready to lose my step-mom that early; she had basically raised me the best she could and did the best she could to be a parent to me. She was my parent. I was not ready to lose her. I had not gained the prospective on life, which I needed in order to be ok if she died at that time. I remember telling her in the hospital that I was happy she didn't die—laughing through the tears I would have never had if not for her making me feel. To this day, as I am almost thirty I thank her for three things in my life:

1. She made me feel.
2. She never made me call her mom.

3. I know she will always love me no
   matter what.

Her choosing to be my parent was a
kindness and she was the greatest step-mom she
could be.

The year before this, my step-aunt had failed
at trying to commit suicide. That occurrence was
triggering because of my own mother's suicide.
However, it also held a realization in me mending
my relationship with my cousin. A cousin that I felt
very connected to and protective.

Time remains a constant even though I am
aware it is relative. There have been times in my
life like high school that now feel like they were a
blink of the eye. Yet the last few years of my
twenties have been some of the more difficult of my
life and feel long and drawn out.

When I was in high school dealing with the
above—dealing with having fickle friends, dealing
with minimally finding out who I was at that time
and who I wanted to be in the future—the people I
remember helping me most were my teachers. To
have a teacher be accused of misconduct, and even
though I hoped it wasn't true and it turned out to not
be true, my heart was breaking and the adults that
were meant to guide me had thoroughly failed.

My senior year in high school was harder
than I knew at the time. My faith in adults was

shaken; I needed help but didn't know how to ask for it. I felt isolated and alone. This wasn't the first time but it felt darker; it felt big. Now I realize how strong I was even then, and I now thank everything that occurred because I knew what suicide did to those I loved, I knew and had the strength to never try to kill myself. Not everyone has the power to have the same thoughts when they are in dark places as I did. Even now, as I enter my thirties, I still have moments of brief responsibility where I notice I have to power to choose life or death.

Time is circular. I come back to the same issues over and over. Friends of mine come back to the same conflicts and patterns over and over. It takes an amazing amount of self awareness and insight and reflection as well as drive and will to change habits and drive your life vehicle down a different road than in the same neighborhood you have always driven around. Make a different choice, if you are feeling stuck. Ask for help from someone if you are feeling like no one.

Along with the issues above one solution came about to an entirely different issue. It came time for me to get a breast reduction and I did it. I was seventeen, a senior in high school, and finally my boobs would be smaller and maybe I wouldn't be noticed as the big boob girl. That was my identifier in high school. The theater girl with big tits. I had never dated or really had a guys show any interest that wasn't tied to my appearance and body. I felt sexualized from a very early age, and as I have described felt like I sold my body to gain friends. To make people like me, because that is the only way I felt I got attention.

It would have been nice if my high school had a class about life not just history. Even better would be a mandatory life class each year in which trained life coaches or therapists would have been around to help and teach about respect. Where they got to know us as kids and figured out how to better help us become adults. Where the impact of my actions and the actions around me were explained in a matter-of-fact manner. Where a teenager whom felt neglected and lost could have expressed her inner thoughts, in a safe controlled space.

One of the teachers and adults who never let me down in high school was the director of the high school musical. He was very loyal to me, he told me when I betrayed his trust, and he never, ever made me feel uncomfortable or taken advantage of; he was a true teacher and respected me more than any other adult had. He treated me with a lot of respect. Probably more respect than I deserved. I felt responsible at times for others, I remember being blamed for my cousin not getting a better role in the musical, and feeling like it was my fault, but that guilt was never placed on me by the person making the decision—always by family. Any time I asked for help this teacher and educator was there as a teacher and educator. He taught me about life in many ways, as did his wife and son. My senior year tested my relationship with this man because I was being traumatized at every turn. We performed the musical chosen by him. Those students that participated in the musical with me are some of the kindest, best people I ever got to know. They all contributed to saving my life, even if at the time they didn't know it.

We live in this great age of technology where thankfully it looks like we as a society are trying to make each other better, lift each other up, and be kind. The more time that goes by the more I realize how much I love talking to others about their lives and about how they overcame their individual struggles. When I sit down to binge TV or Netflix or Disney or Amazon Prime I find myself drawn to a multitude of shows, about knowledge, gore, love, sex, war, family, comedy, perseverance, resilience, coming of age, science, humanity, time, fiction, magic, and religion. My interests are endless and always have been. There is a certain amount of freedom in art. Art promotes freedom.

7. FREEDOM

When we reach the age of eighteen, or sometimes nineteen or sometimes other ages, a pivotal time in our life comes up. We get to the end of high school and make the choice to pursue college or not. We are sent out into the world on our own. I personally loved going away to college. It was the next step. It was the transition to autonomy. It hopefully would challenge me in new exciting ways. It was an experience that I had been told about since I was little. My two sisters went to college; one took a gap year. As far as I was concerned that was the next step. At the time I made the choice but I also knew it was expected of me. The pressure was there of my own volition but I didn't see many other options and if I'm honest, I wanted the experience, I wanted the growth; I wanted someone to break through my walls and hoped higher education could do it.

There was another layer to this want as well. Up until now my life had been lived as the third child. Then when my step-mom came into the picture I was the fifth child. I was the last. I often didn't get what my other siblings got. I didn't get a bat mitzvah. I didn't pursue gymnastics. I didn't have great birthdays. I didn't have friends. I didn't even get into trouble because I was too responsible. Don't get me wrong, I know I had privilege but I never felt like a kid. I always felt measured by my choices.

My sister brought home friends from college when I was seventeen and I hung out with them, prevented us from getting arrested outside my house, then helped clean up vomit because one of the boys threw up on someone else's head. My parents treated me kind of like an adult before I was one.

Maybe I would find love in college like my sisters and finally feel whole. Maybe I would get into a bit of trouble. There was so much want and desire going into college, and starting my freedom journey to figure out the human I was going to be and wanted to be. At the time, I didn't know this; I didn't know I was seeking my own approval. I didn't know I wanted to push my own limits. I didn't know I wanted to find myself; I just knew I wanted to choose college.

After high school I went off to be a counselor at a sleep away camp. The same camp I went to when I was a kid. At the time it felt pre-determined. As a kid I had idealized the counselors at camp. I saw them having so much fun. They seemed like they knew who they were. They were my heroes because they were the only ones who, I felt, ever paid attention to me. During the summers from age seven to sixteen I would spend –one-to-two months at the camp. Those summers were my first tastes of freedom. They are where I experienced plenty of experiences that were good and bad. Sleep away camp provided the opportunity for me to test-drive my capabilities to make choices both growing up and as an adult. I did the best I could to make the right choices. That first summer I was a counselor I also had my first consensual sexual experiences with someone I really liked. He was the first guy I ever sort of dated but I chose to not have sex with him. He pursued me, and yet there was some darkness in that relationship. Some trust lost, and important lessons learned.

Freshman year was interesting. I tried to find my place in the program I got into. It was really hard. I never had friends that stuck in high school and now in college I felt like an outsider. Being the outsider was surprisingly easy. I refused to go to parties and no one tried hard enough to get to know me. Eventually one girl decided she wanted to become my friend. She was the first friend I really remember having as an adult. My hesitation to allow her to get close to me was a caution. At the time I was paralyzed by the fear of getting close to her and her leaving me, or not liking me, or any number of horrifying thoughts. The proximity was intoxicating. This freedom was also the first year of dating that I experienced. I was on all the dating sites, JDate, Plenty of Fish, and OkCupid. Tinder wasn't around yet. I was desperate to find someone to love me. What I didn't realize at the time was that I could love me and I should be looking for people who will allow me to love them how I like to love.

After my first year in college I went back to being a camp counselor. I was still a virgin and I still had such abandonment blocks. The bubble environment of that second summer as a counselor would facilitate me losing my virginity, which at the time was a non-event in my eyes. Yet looking back it was more important as a rite of passage that I hold dear in the path to me figuring out how I make choices. It wasn't special. At the time I liked that is wasn't a big deal.

Our society places such a high value on sex. I wish it didn't. However later I started to hold sex in two separate categories, which I will discuss. When I was nineteen however, I just wanted to experience it. I had been exposed to sex early in life by talking about it. I started exploring my own body early. Then, entering puberty I became interested in what my body could do. Yet society told me sex was wrong. Sex was dirty. Sex was evil. I couldn't understand this, if sex was so bad then why did my body make me feel so good when I participated in sexual acts, either with myself or with others? Logically I knew I had a right to choose and do with my body what I wanted. Emotionally, sex was much more complicated.

When I was younger I always knew looks were a different kind of currency. I saw the attention pretty people got, and envied it. The envy stemmed from wanting to have others pay attention to me. From a young age I got attention for my breasts and their size. I didn't know enough about my own needs, to see I was selling my body for likes as a kid, in an age before I realized the value of wanting to be accepted for who I am and what I am, I didn't have high standards for the attention I received. Wanting to be wanted can be a powerful motivator to do actions you do not want to do. I didn't know that I saw sex as a way to get others to like me.

The guy I lost my virginity to was not someone I loved. He was someone I chose. I was not particularly attracted to him, but could tell he was attracted to me. He was my boss. He slowly endeared himself to me, and at times pushed my boundaries. Later in life I regarded that relationship as not the best because I was unaware of prior sex abuse, but he served his purpose of being my first.

Growing up I had heard of women losing their virginity as this big event. They built it up and maybe it went well, but sometimes it was traumatic and now I was nineteen and I didn't want a big event. I didn't want trauma. I wanted to choose; I wanted someone I felt comfortable with, someone whom I knew loved women's bodies. I wanted someone I could have sex with a lot and figure out what I liked and not be self conscious during the process. The man I lost my virginity to didn't know he was my first; he never asked. The way I talked about sex and the way I carried myself, I doubt he would ever suspect that he was my first. Later in life, I won't say the experience was perfect, but in my eyes, I'm not sure I would have changed it. It was one of the first times in my life I felt I was making a choice that I clearly wanted to make. I wanted him to be my first. I wanted to use him as much as he was using me.

The one thing that I remember being off about my first time was that he wouldn't kiss me. Later I found out this was a boundary for him. He didn't like kissing because it was far more intimate then the act of sex in his eyes. What I didn't know about myself is that I had previously felt like a prostitute as a kid, trying to sell my body so peers would like me. When we started sleeping together the prior abuse caused me to have panic attacks because of past trauma. This wasn't his fault, but he probably should have treated me better; he should have allowed for more compassion. At the time, I didn't know any better. I accepted less than I deserved, because I was desperate.

Sophomore year started and I really realized I hated school. The program I was in wasn't the best atmosphere. I struggled to get noticed and find guidance. Looking back on most of my schooling I never felt challenged; I didn't have a lot of motivation and the value of education was not properly described or presented in a way that forced me to understand what education is and its purpose. I had a head of my program who challenged me personally but academically I didn't feel challenged. My stubborn nature was frustrated at the personal challenge and lack of academic challenge. Midway through the first semester of my sophomore year I missed the passion I had for a specific sector of theater that made me feel alive. I felt restless and I missed music. I was feeling complacent. This year at college was also the first year I was sexually active in college. It was also the first time I felt sexually violated and was aware of the abuse. The decision to transfer had nothing to do with sex though; I missed musical theater, and decided to transfer schools. I also decided to do an internship that summer between sophomore and junior year. I wanted to start my career. I wanted to feel useful.

Summer came and I had acquired an internship at a summer stock theater. I remember going after this internship. Needing this internship. There wasn't anything in my life I wanted more up until this point. I found this theater and I wanted nothing more than to work for them. I went after this opportunity. There was a feeling I had like I was meant to work there. The wish came true. Perseverance paid off. The Long Island adventure started, and little did I know, that first summer really made me grow. I fell in love that summer. Not a successful love. A love that made me grow. A love that made me see that love is not easy—but very complicated if it isn't right.

My parents also were in the middle of figuring out how to be without kids. This was rough on me. My dad was in charge of transferring money for school. I remember one night I went to register for classes, and found out my dad had not transferred money. Then I confronted him about how disappointing it was that he dropped the ball. He then told me my step-mom was threatening to divorce him. This was the first time I remember standing up for myself to my father verbally. I remember telling him that them getting a divorce was none of my business, and how dare he tell me that this was somehow my fault. His marriage was not my responsibility. Although looking back if they had gotten a divorce, I know I would have felt responsible. I was nervous over starting a new school. Everything felt like a new beginning. I was angry my dad had let me down.

Junior year. New school. Unrequited love. I went back to start a new school unable to stop thinking about a man I had fallen in love with over the summer. My heart felt like there should be a song or two from Grease playing in the background. The new school wasn't all I thought. Half way through this year I thought I had made a huge mistake and almost tried to transfer back to the first school.

For the first time since my breast reduction, my step-mom was a parent to me. I remember crying on the phone in my car, saying I wanted to transfer back and my step-mom said "NO! Finish school where you are; that's the easiest route to be done. That's the end goal. To finish." She was right. My friend that I had made at my first school was gradually becoming less of friend no matter how much I tried to keep her; she showed me that if I stopped trying we wouldn't be friends at all. Which happened. The people in the program at my new school hated me because I threatened their place at the school. They saw me as a threat and I felt so alone. I found an internship for my second semester of my junior year.

The internship I got was partially due to a family member having a contact at an institution where they performed ballet. It was in the education department and this was the first place I experienced discrimination against kids. This discrimination was ultimately quite traumatic as I look back at it. I remember witnessing adults making fun of the pictures kids sent to the institution. I remember not feeling like I belonged and I remember them stating I did an awful job even though I showed up every day did what was asked of me; they felt I wasn't excited about my environment. I didn't know at the time that this was wrong. My GPA for that semester was shot. I felt worthless, though I will admit that I did my best at the time. It was an internship after all. The embarrassment I had over that poor grade was extensive. The shame I had was crushing.

Summer came along and I went back to the same theater as the previous summer. I didn't have the same experience as the previous year. This was the first time I remember feeling wanted. Halfway through the summer I came across a man that was beautiful. He had a girlfriend, and so I knew he wasn't a man I would have any potential with. To want another human to be sexual with you is a weird thing but I came across someone I wanted for nothing more than sex. He was not someone I would ever love, and sometimes I didn't even like him. He was beautiful and he wanted me. He pursued me. It was empowering, if short lived. It was summer. Realizing I had pity for him was helpful in understanding how to respect his choice to cheat on his girlfriend. Honesty was always important to me, but respect feeds honesty. He didn't respect himself and therefore lost my respect, but I still chose to have a sexual fling. If there had been consequences, I would have endured them. Let me be clear. I never wanted his girlfriend to find out, and as far as I know she didn't.

Sleeping with men who were attached has happened a few times in my adult sexual life. Respect is something I hold on levels, and I respect all the choices others make, including the choice to be dishonest to one's spouse. Before I ever sleep with a man who I know has a wife or a girlfriend I ask one question that lets me know what type of person they are, "Does she know?" If the guy answers that his significant other does not know, then I now know this man is dishonest and all he is good for is sex. Friendship is a possibility, but even in friendship I know he can be dishonest, so trust will always be less-than. I have never cheated on anyone I was dating, but that's mostly because I have never been in a true monogamous relationship.

Senior year started and I needed to overload my schedules both semesters in order to finish school and get my degree. The decision to assist on shows and not be the head manager was a great choice. Looking back this was the first time I truly felt challenged in school. Because I had overloaded my schedule and created no time for me to procrastinate. **I was forced to test my abilities and manage my time.** I received all A's and B's my senior year, and one C in Hebrew but I remember being immensely proud of myself in academics for the first time since high school. The pride I felt in high school was hardly ever about academics. Skating through high school, it was more about my work in theater. Theater was the first place I felt I belonged. It was the first place I felt powerful and not helpless or worthless. The theater was the first place I gave and earned respect. Theater was my education, but then I made it my career.

8. Respect

Respect is very important socially. We are constantly told to respect each other, our friends, our family, our teachers, our elders, our parents, ourselves. Respect is subjective. It means something different to each person that speaks the word. It is not something with a clear definition. We are constantly being told to show respect but it is also something to be earned. There are varying levels of respect.

Growing up I always challenged authority. This stems from the absolute knowledge I had that all adults do not always know best. My mother was an adult and she should have been an authority in my life. Instead, she disrespected her life and my life by ending her life. My sisters and I always challenged authority because we were desperate to make it known that respect is not blindly given. We were desperate for people to respect us.

Here is a journal entry from a social media platform that I will discuss later called Fetlife that helps break down different types of respect:

<u>Respect and the Power of Silence</u>

Growing up I wasn't really taught what respect was. I didn't understand boundaries or when it was appropriate to tell someone to be quiet or whether asking someone to be quiet was disrespectful. I was always so quiet because I didn't know how to respect myself while respecting others.

It's subjective really. Everyone may have a different definition of what being respectful means and what being disrespectful means. Is it really subjective though? Certain things are outright disrespectful—any kind of touching without permission or interrupting someone while they are talking—but could a group even agree on those points?

In relationships of all kinds, how do you properly approach respect? It isn't universal. Something I find disrespectful could be justified by that person in terms of them respecting their personal needs. I guess when talking about respect you need to identify the different kinds that come to mind.

Basic respect: the respect you show every human, even if they disrespect you.

Physical respect: respect of your body and others' bodies.

Personal respect: respecting someone in your personal life and their personal views and personal values.

Professional respect: respecting that someone can do their job/follow procedure/lead by example/doesn't do the bare minimum/completes tasks as assigned and speaks up when needed if knowledge is required to complete tasks given.

Sexual respect: respecting sexual preferences in relation to dating and sexual orientation or sexual preferences. What they like to be called during sex, their sexual lifestyle, not judging them for liking something sexually that you do not like. Asking before assuming.

Verbal respect: not interrupting someone while talking/admiring the way someone speaks/not correcting vernacular unless prompted. Calling someone by the name they want to be called.

Emotional respect: validating a person's feelings and not making them feel bad for having the emotions they are experiencing. Realizing emotional trauma is just as damaging as physical trauma.

Respect for others' thought process: recognizing that not everyone thinks the same/patience with others questions. Having the respect to ask questions to someone when they don't make sense, or talk about themselves with ambiguity.

Having any relationship is hard but having the forethought to put emphasis on respecting each other certainly helps to set boundaries which help with fear and protecting yourself from being harmed. I appreciate that emphasis. I struggle and thrive at practicing the above respects in my lifestyle. However, when should my self respect override the respect that I'm supposed to be showing my fellow human/prospective relationship/friend/family/lover? When does silence become disrespectful to yourself?

Recently I figured out that self respect is like building a house for yourself. The foundation can be built by nature but I believe it is mostly built by those that socially influence our personalities and our choices. When you meet others that you respect you start building a house together by making a choice to show them more than basic respect and the other person has hopefully shown you they can respect your choices. You then order your materials to start the foundation for that relationship with mutual respect. As you get the foundation built, you start having more and more choices you need to make to determine what kind of house you want to build. You have to be willing to show each other mutual respect though, to have a say in these choices. Choices after college would help me create new rooms in my own house.

College was over and I originally thought I would return to the theater I had worked at the previous two summers, but I was told there was no position for me. I was devastated. All I wanted at the time was to work at this theater. The producer at the company told me that there was no position for me. Later I found out that this was false. They hired someone else for the position that I had thought would be mine and the producer didn't have enough respect for me to tell me.

Bouncing back from that disappointment was not an easy task and I ended up moving to Washington D.C. to be an apprentice at a local theater. After college I became very hard on myself and wanted to find someone to love. I wanted to find someone to help me build my house. My self worth was fixated on finding people to love me—fixated on trying to gain self respect with others helping me. At the time I thought it was about finding someone to fill the hole in my heart and feel less abandoned. I was looking for my fairy tale. There was a need for me to get over the love I felt for the guy I was in love with back in college. I had always wanted to live in D.C. because it is our capital and it was enticing to change things up and challenge myself; I thought maybe I could find love there. Maybe someone would want to keep me company.

Housing was provided but the pay was abysmal. After three months I was over D.C. It is a city that changes drastically every few years, but hates change. People are set in their ways. It was also the first time I tried speed dating, which resulted in a six-month-long delusional relationship and where the guy wouldn't let me into his imaginary house. He was studying to be a doctor, and I was enthralled with and had a lot of respect for him because he knew how to respect himself. I could have fallen in love and married him then and there. He was kind and the first penis I had ever experienced that was uncircumcised. He took the time to teach me, and I gained a lot of sexual knowledge from him, but it was never going to last, because I didn't know how to respect myself yet. He was not interested in something long term at the time. At least he had enough respect to tell me; I just didn't have enough respect to listen. At least he taught me a few tricks. We actually stayed in touch and he is married now. I am immensely happy for him. Even more so, I am immensely appreciative of the respect he showed me and taught me at that time in my life.

After the speed dating, I met a man at a bar. We dated for a total of two months. He did not understand respect, and for the first time in my life **I remember having a clear understanding of that concept**. He was toxic and volatile, and he put me in danger. This was my jumping-off point to understanding respect and finding my own path of understanding as to how to treat others and myself with respect. This was where I ordered my materials for my own house and decided I was going to build a house for myself. I knew exactly what I wanted it to look like and I could clearly show others how to respect me, and how I would respect them. He didn't understand his disrespect and I ended the relationship with him. This volatile man had another profound effect on my life. His mom was bi-polar and he was not stable; he had manic episodes. However, for the first time I realized maybe my life was better without my mom.

9. Unexpected

After D.C., I went upstate New York to spend a summer in 2013 working for a company that did workshops for a lot of Broadway productions. This job was a paying position and a big role for me in my career. The summer was a giant unexpected growing process, which is ironic because the main objective, as I understood it at the time, was for the creative teams of prospective shows to present workshop versions for the season in order to grow their show. It was a company devoted to growth—creatively and individually. I didn't see it at the time, but it was a company devoted to respect. Little did I know this summer would be the **first time I got confirmation verbally that I needed to examine myself and who I was and how I treated others**.

That summer was the first time I ever had people working as my subordinates. They were a group of four interns of different walks of life and now, years later, I don't remember anything I did to warrant the reactions I got from them, but the reactions had a profound effect. They made me reexamine who I was and who I wanted to be, not just in theater but also in life. It made me realize I am not always kind or respectful and that affects people.

The last thing I wanted was to belittle people or feel like I had treated someone unfairly. I wanted to be stern and liked. I wanted to be a manager people would come to with problems and not someone they would go around and dread. I wanted to be respected and to respect them in return. I didn't want to make issues worse. I wanted to be there for those that worked under me. Most of all I wanted people to accept me for who I was, not who they perceived me to be. I was trying way too hard, and I was way too unaware of my limitations at the time.

Leaving Poughkeepsie at the end of the summer, I was moving to NYC. Broadway was in my sights, and I had acquired an internship with a prominent Broadway general management company. There were no words for how excited I was, and to top it off, my oldest sister and her husband had offered for me to live with them. This was unexpected.

The idea that I would be living with family while I started what I hoped would lead to my dreams coming true truly was amazing. To have a built-in support system was wonderful. I remember being in awe when I worked at my first GM production company. The learning was nonstop and I realized this was what I wanted to do. I wanted to be like the general managers of this Broadway Show. I wanted to command respect and make decisions. I wanted to have choices. I wanted to help people experience theater like I had experienced it when I was a kid.

Moving into the city, I was a bit scared. The only thing I could do was my best and I knew that. That would all change after the six months I spent working for this wonderful show. This was the first time in my career that I experienced true envy and jealousy in my work.

When the internship was over, one of my fellow interns received a position with the company. He went on to rise and now has the job I always wanted. At the time I did that internship, all I wanted was to be a company manager on Broadway. They are the epicenter of a show. They deal with finances and marketing and make a lot of choices with the guidance of a general manager, depending on their experience.

After the internship I went on to do a management associate position and then another internship for another long-running Broadway show. I was planning to turn this internship into what I wanted the previous one to be. I would say no to nothing. Do everything that was asked of me, and seek out projects. It wasn't until much later in life I realized I was not proactive enough. I was slightly entitled and a bit naïve, and mostly disrespectful to myself. Green. I was green. There was a huge part of me that thought I could get by because that's what I had been doing up until this point. Then I got a phone call and everything changed.

The call came in on a Tuesday. On the other end was a manager from a cruise line. He said we had gone to the same colleges and offered me a Company Manager position on one of their largest cruise ships at the time. The thoughts "Is he messing with me?" and "Is this real?" were swirling in my head. How was it that I was getting this opportunity because of the colleges I went to? I felt fear but also excitement. At last another dream could come true: I was going to get paid to travel. How cool is that? It was certainly unexpected. The excitement was enormous.

Six days later, after doing the impossible and getting medically cleared, I was on ship. In order to work on a ship a person has to do all sorts of medical pre-requisites. This includes a pap smear for women, which I thought was outrageous. However, now after working on a ship, I get it. They are taking responsibility for each one of its crew members medically and therefore they need to know as much about each crew member as possible, medically speaking, in case emergencies happen and they need to medically treat a crew member.

My first day on a giant floating city was one of the most memorable experiences. To be flown down to Port Canaveral Florida and then picked up by a private transport—it was the first time in my life I felt important. Getting on the ship was a bit of a blur. I remember leaving something in my bag and then almost getting lost, and finally meeting the man that I would be taking over for in five days. This was my first cruise ship and all I had was five days to learn my position and learn as much as I could about this atmosphere and environment. I have always been a fast learner. I remember telling myself "I got this" a lot.

Thankfully this was not my first bubble environment. Summer stock theater had prepared me for ship life, but some of the experiences I was about to come across were brand new and would be quite challenging. **These challenges would shape me and change me in ways even I couldn't foresee**.

That first day on that ship I met a man that would change my life. A man whom I would fall in and then fall out of love with. A man whom every day, for then after I would be grateful for meeting because he catapulted me into the person I am now. All because of Love.

10. Love

Love may be the most complicated, abstract thing a human brain comes to know. That is if you get to know what Love truly means. Everyone has a different definition of Love. This was made clear more recently as a friend is writing a book about love and we talked at length about how people have all sorts of differing answers to about love. Definitions of love are as diverse as those whom I have asked. The differences in people's perspectives of love are part of why the concept is so beautiful.

When it comes to my brain and the way I perceive love, there are different categories of love and different emotions, wants, needs, and expectations that go along with each category and strength of love. I have always been very scientific about love. I believe it can be measured and quantified. I believe there are markers—tests or experiments that can be run to see if it exists.

When I view love I see it as a bar graph. On the left side you have percentage of 1 to infinity, is there ever such a thing as too much love. Once I reach 100 in any category I know I accept someone 100% in that category, and then my love can only grow. Then each bar could represent a different type of love.

Genuinely I am surprised I don't have a passage on love already. My definition of love has been fairly stationary since I fell in love and was loved back by someone romantically. However, recently I have been exploring different types of love, and how they relate to each other.

Love without sub-categories is hard to describe. It is emotion, and something we cannot see but know exists. It is a want to accept the good, bad, and the weird—all of what makes someone who they are as a human, or animal, or object. You can love anything and that anything may have faults and imperfections. It's about seeing with your eyes, heart, and mind that this love is what it is and not wishing it was something else but understanding it can change. Respecting differing perceptions of love is a part of loving yourself and others.

Human Love is the recognition of your own absolute acceptance and knowledge of another person regardless of likes or dislikes in that moment. However, human love is also reliant on the other person being honest with themselves and showing you who they are, so you can accurately know them. In order to have a love for a human you need to know enough about them in order to know one way or the other if you love them. If you don't know what qualities in another human you value, how can you know you love them? A better question is: If you don't know what qualities you yourself value, how do you know when you have seen those qualities in another human?

Object Love is the recognition of your love for an object. There is a want or need for the object and sentimental connection to an object because it elicits feelings and strong emotional connection. Objects are not capable of making choices and therefore cannot love you back.

Cordial Love is the basic love a person can have for all living things or a basic respect and acceptance of someone's perceived morals and ethics. Humanitarians have a cordial love for all humans. A cordial person might be the polite person who says hello to any stranger who says hello. As an example I have a cordial love for any human I meet that shows me the least amount of respect. I also consider myself a humanitarian. All humans fascinate me and I love the cognitive abilities we possess while we figure out who we want to be.

Romantic Love has a sexual component involved. This love has a driving force that is sex driven, and can be driven to have kids or a family but the most basic attraction and dividing connection is a sexual connection based on pleasure.

Friends or Asexual Love can be just as deep as romantic love but with no sexual desire or component. Friends can move into other types of love, which will not diminish the friendship love.

A person can be in love with their best friend. The main difference between loving someone and being in love with someone is a person's willingness to compromise themselves for the other person. Love, can be unconditional, is reserved for special people in a person's inner circle. Believing in love at first sight has not been my experience. There is power and gravity of choosing someone else's needs over your own needs in the name of love, making the choice to put someone else's need above your own is when love switched from being conditional to unconditional.

Let me paint you a picture. Love can be a rabbit with arms and opposable thumbs. The rabbit can wear hats or pieces of clothing for different types of love. When a rabbit wants to be in love it can make a balloon appear and then hand it to other rabbits to trust it in their care, that they will not let go of the balloon. A rabbit can change its fur as its self love changes, but when a rabbit loves itself for the rabbit it is, it will stop changing its fur. My love rabbit can put on as many layers as it likes and hand out as many in love balloons as it wants.

Loving myself and falling in love with myself was a really rough and long process because for the longest time, I thought I was unlovable. I thought I wasn't worthy of love. I thought no one would ever love me even if they said they did because my mother killed herself and I couldn't for the longest time understand why or how she could do that if love was real. It took me many, many years to start loving myself. If my mother hadn't killed herself I am not sure my self love would have been in jeopardy; however, her suicide also showed me how much power love can give as well.

This brings me to Familial Love. Recently I have realized that there is a point where love goes deeper—that unconditional love is a familial love. Whether someone is biologically related to you or not, when a person unconditionally loves you, they will chose to put your needs above their own if presented with that choice. To this day I understand that my mother loved me so much that she thought she was putting my needs above her own. She believed that I, along with my sisters, were better off in this world without her. This realization was hard to come by and only happened when I fell head over heels in love with someone myself. I fell so in love with this person that the only way I knew I loved him more than I loved myself was because he once said to me "If I am not in a better place in my life by the time I'm thirty-five, I'll kill myself".

In that moment I remember physically wanting to run. I wanted to run in the other direction because how could I stay knowing he may choose to kill himself and leave me alone. He would be one more person to leave me and make me feel not enough and like I was nothing. He was one more person to abandon me. I stayed because I was in love with him, and at my core I wanted him to choose me, but instead I chose him. I wanted him to pick me. I wanted him to stay because he loved me.

I wanted him to be my mother and not make the choice she made. Looking back at this now, it is so clear that the connection that I felt for him was entangled with my need to repair my worth in relation to my mother's suicide. My love for him was respecting my own needs, but he was disrespecting his and mine by not seeing how he disrespected his own will to live.

This relationship happened on my first ship. I fell in love in a bubble environment and it was wonderful. It wasn't easy though. We had a few ups and downs, but I chose him. He had his own issues and didn't think he was worthy of me, and told me often. The problem with him telling me this is it was disrespectful in its entirety to me. He was trying to choose for me that I was too good for him. I had all this love to give him and I wanted to give it unconditionally. I couldn't understand why he wouldn't let me love him. At the time I accepted him for exactly who he was. All I wanted was for him to choose me too, to love me too. To respect my choice in loving him. I didn't realize how much pressure I was putting on myself, or on him.

That ship contract was the hardest and best time of my life. What came after was even harder. I had fallen in love with a man that was much different than what I expected. At first when I met him he wasn't even someone I thought I liked. I was sexually attracted to him but I didn't think he had long-term potential. He had me convinced for two weeks he had been incarcerated. Which once I knew wasn't true made me like him even more. He was messing with me—he hadn't been. I chose to fall in love with him. I remember making the choice. I chose to fall out of love with him, and I remember making that choice. He was intelligent and fair, or so he thought. He changed my mind about a few things and that wasn't something at the time that was easy. He taught me the respect that happens when someone shows you new information. He was good for me, in the long run, if not damaging to me at the time.

Love for me is a choice. It is the choice of acceptance. The choice to listen. The choice to stay. The choice to respect another person. It is all about choices and knowledge and opportunity. Loving yourself is no different, but it can be harder, because with others you can escape if you don't agree with their choices or don't like them but still love them. With yourself, the love you have for yourself is all about knowing yourself. There is no opportunity to escape from yourself and that can be maddening. It is about choosing to get to know how your brain works and getting to the root of where your feelings come from and what they mean. Love is not instantaneous. It can happen quickly if people are open and honest about who they are, but make no mistake in my eyes: love is absolutely a choice that is a driving force and for me it keeps me alive every day.

11. Depression

That first professional contract making a descent living was over. I thought I had found the love of my life–the person that was going to make me feel worthy of love. At the time, I didn't know I needed that from him. I didn't know that my self worth was as fragile as it was, but I still hadn't dealt with my feelings of inadequacy. I didn't realize the pressure I was putting on him. I felt guilty over not being enough to save my mother from killing herself. I didn't know suicide was a choice every person has, and if they chose to kill themselves then it does not mean they don't love you. It means any number of different things to different people and most of the time we don't get answers. I didn't understand mental illness or how our brains physically work in the way I do now, years later.

After leaving my first ship, I fell into the deepest depression I had ever experienced. I was twenty-four and I remember getting off the ship, thinking that as long as I hold onto this love I will be ok. I will have something to lift me out of the dark when it gets dark. When the world feels unbearably awful and I can't see the good, this love will be my light. I get why people need god, but god has never been tangible or something that came through for me. This love I knew was real. The issue was that even if I knew it was real, he didn't know and I needed to tell him.

Two weeks after I got off the ship he got off the ship. This was the first time I was going to say "I Love You" to someone who was not my family, and it was the first time I meant it in the way of a long-term love. I wanted to have babies with this man and love him for the rest of my life but knew he was scared, I knew he wasn't going to say it back. I was saying it for me. I was saying it to show him the respect of knowing for sure that I loved him. To acknowledge out loud that I accepted him for who he was—exactly who he was—and I didn't care if he said it back. I knew at the time I said it to him he loved me back but his trauma—his life— was preventing him from making the choice to say it back. He was scared.

The next four-to-six months were agony. We emailed back and forth; I was out of work because I had turned down a contract on a smaller ship because of my ego. I slipped into a deep depression because I felt I had no purpose. I took some classes. I did some soul searching. I read a lot of books. I felt I was waiting around to hear from him.

The loneliness I felt was drowning me. I felt helpless and I felt like my mind was betraying me. How could I go from loving and being so happy with this man, to thinking I had made all the feelings up and was delusional by thinking that he loved me?

Looking back, I still had so much to learn about myself—about who I was and who I would become. The world felt dark and unfair. It felt like I didn't belong and had no purpose. No matter how hard I tried I couldn't shake these feelings. I had to then take a hard look at what led to these feelings of worthlessness. This is when I took action.

Logically speaking I knew even at this time that killing myself was not an option. There were people in my life that I loved too much to even consider taking that step or action. I didn't want to cause them any more pain or wonder or feel like they were not enough or responsible. My love and need to not hurt others and make them sad is the driving force behind why I chose to stay and fight for my own life—for my own happiness—and to try to do a little good, at least for myself. Finding a way to understand why I kept coming back to thoughts of suicide became of the utmost importance at this time.

At twenty-five, I felt uneducated in myself. I felt I needed definitions of concepts that had been talked about to me all my life but I didn't actually know what they meant. I needed a better foundation for my life to help me survive when hurt came along. I wanted to know why it was that I kept wanting to not live, but knew I couldn't deprive my loved ones of time with me. I needed to find a better way to exist and I needed to educate myself on my own mind.

I needed my own Mental Armor to prevent the hurt that was so apparently a part of life and living. I needed protection from those who like me didn't see the hurt they could mentally inflict on others. I needed to strengthen my mind and my mental health to provide for the healthy life I always was working toward.

At first when I truly started to examine myself, the stream of things people had always told me felt like unnecessary noise. The positives didn't like coming up to the forefront of my mind. I wasn't sure who I wanted to be and I didn't know how to get there. Maybe I needed to start with who I ***didn't*** want to be. I looked up books about self esteem, and how to get more confidence. I started reading books about psychology. I started looking up all the definitions of things people my whole life had told me I needed to do in order to live a healthier and happier life. I felt inadequate; I felt lost; I felt insignificant; I felt worthless. I had realized there was something wrong and I needed to work to fix it. I needed to fix my brain and the way I thought about myself and try to understand where these thoughts and feelings stemmed from before moving forward. I needed to create a history and start fixing wounds.

Looking back, it's like I had a broken bone only it wasn't a bone—it was my mind. I had tried to put band aids on my mind and to no avail; I was still depressed and had immense anxiety. It's like every time my brain bone started healing I hit it against something and it broke again. The amount of times my brain has felt broken feels insurmountable, and all along I was just looking for my Mental Armor.

The first book I came across that really helped was Nathaniel Brandon's *The Six Pillars of Self Esteem*. This was the first step to figuring out what self esteem was, and why I was lacking it. As I read, there were light bulbs after light bulbs that came on. I finished the book and was empowered to work on myself even more. I had found some answers, and I found them on my own. This was probably the first time I felt like my own psychological hero. ***Like I had gathered a small piece of armor.***

The work that followed was hard. My world had been cracked open and I was working to build it up and get to the route of why these bouts of depression kept happening. **I was becoming my own therapist—my own advocate**. We are raised in a culture where saying we are wrong or owning up to a poor reaction or simply saying "I don't know" is not a positive answer. Mental illness itself is looked upon with disgust and stigma. I thought I was crazy—that I had made this love up. The truth is powerful and necessary to bring us back down to earth and reality. The man I loved finally admitted he loved me back. I felt vindicated and calm because what I thought I knew was true and I wasn't delusional. Little did I know that love was not enough.

12. Second Chances

After this realization came another. I had
been too hasty in turning down an opportunity to go
on a smaller ship because of pride and my ego. How
did I know I wouldn't like this other job—this other
ship–unless I tried it? The job was in a theater and
at the time my purpose in life was to help others
through theater and this would help me. It meant
having to admit I was wrong. Leading up to this
point I never had trouble taking responsibility for
myself, but I remember this experience humbling
me greatly.

After reading the books I had read, I knew I
had made some decisions too hastily. Now I needed
to take responsibility for my mistake and try. Try to
do better. Treat others better. Continue to work on
myself and work through what made me tick. There
is a part of me now that realizes I was obsessed with
finding out my true motivations. To owning up to
the mistakes I had made and doing a job I once
thought was my passion and always would be.

Going back on ship I had a goal. I was going
to go in with an open mind; I was going to have fun,
and maybe this would take my mind off the
loneliness I still felt and the rejection and separation
from someone I loved. Maybe it could help me to
feel like I was making a difference and provide for

distraction from the world we live in. After all, this was why I got into theater—to help people—even if when I made this decision, I was ultimately just trying to help myself.

Research has shown how entertainment, and specifically theater, can be therapeutic. For me, I loved the adrenaline that happens when working on a show. I love the organizational aspects and the unified experience. More research has shown that audience members heartbeat rhythms synchronize during performances. I have physically felt the effects of energy in the room and it helped make me feel less alone. It helps calm me. It helps to feel a part of something. It helps me feel like I have a purpose. I craved these feelings within my work.

Going back on a ship was my answer then; it gave me something to do while I waited for the man I loved to fix himself and deem himself worthy of me. *A little note to anyone who has a man tell them they deserve better, listen to them.* My experience on the first ship wasn't exactly a walk in the park, and going back was nerve-wracking as well. I had fallen in love yes, but the culture on Cruise Liners for female employees and specifically managers, is complicated and socially challenging.

The bubble environment is exacerbated. This second contract, my eyes were truly opened to the silencing culture of cruise ship life. I wasn't strong enough at the time to really make a difference but I also did not stay quiet. I tried to then use my voice to help others if I could.

The first half of my second contract was great. I had a female boss who said to me something I will never forget. She told me I didn't need to be so damaged by my past experiences. Her exact words were **"You are more than your TRAUMA."** I had a choice to move forward from them; I just had to make the conscious choice too. I had to build my Mental Armor up and beat back mental illness. That's not verbatim; it's what I remember, but looking back I needed her to say that to me and I am eternally grateful of the manager she was in that situation. At the time I thought it was a bit crass and slightly condescending, but it was true and I respected her for saying it to my face. She was trying to help me and it took about six years to see it, but she definitely did help. Unfortunately, she was only around for a small period of time when I was there. She continued to be someone I admired and years later I am so grateful for her small contribution to my life.

At the time, I was craving a female figure to show me success—to show me *I wasn't my trauma*. She was the first woman to ever tell me that—to ever support me in a way I hadn't experienced before. At the time I couldn't understand it, but now I like to think that she meant I can be more than the trauma I've endured. This woman was more influential to me than I knew at the time. She was my hero. She was amazing and I am so happy we had that interaction.

Then came my first true experience being diminished and degraded for being a strong woman. The man that replaced the woman who was my boss was a misogynist and a truly awful leader. He was so disrespectful. It was the first time in my life I had been singled out for being female. This boss did not want to hear me talk. He didn't want me to do my job, and he constantly belittled and degraded me without my consent. He was a "Yes" man. He wanted me to simply say yes to everything he said, wanted, or asked for, and to follow orders. It was maddening to feel so insignificant and feel like not only did I not have a voice, but also that I saw this man having relationships with multiple women from different cliques; this wasn't my business but I worried about these women getting taken advantage of by him. He was smart and had an ego the size of Texas and he was a liar. At the time, my sexual ideals were narrower, but I highly doubted that this man was being honest with these women because he had shown me his true character, and I hated him at the time. Now I am thankful for the experience as it makes it easier to spot these types of men.

One day, one of the other ships had an emergency in their entertainment department. Their production shows had to be cancelled and they needed an entertainer from our ship. I was friends with the manager in my position on that ship; we met every week to give each other support because our positions were unique and having each other was nice. We also got confused for one another a lot as we had similar names. She was fierce and when I got her call I sprang into action. I asked if they had contacted my Cruise Director, the misogynist, and they stated they had tried everything and now were coming to me. They were desperate. Within an a few hours I had come up with a plan, contacted the talent, talked with shore side, and had looped in all relevant parties including copying my boss on all correspondence; however, he was out of the loop because he could not be reached. As soon as he came back into the fold he berated me, admonished me, and told me how little power I had. I had trouble not laughing in his face at his hurt ego when he then told me I wasn't a team player.

Looking back, I gave him too much power. Experience did come out of working with this man. I then went on to warn three other women that would work with this man in my position. I told them everything they needed to know. "Say yes to everything he asks for even if you disagree. He will hang himself, and has a fragile ego and can't handle a woman speaking logic or truth to him because he is illogical." Each one of the women I warned came back to me and said that they were eternally grateful for my advice, and if I hadn't given it they would have wanted to murder him, figuratively speaking. Pride cannot begin to describe the feeling when you make someone else's life easier by telling them the truth and helping them for no other reason.

Leaving that second contract, I already had a third lined up and I was about to take a trip to Europe that I planned while on ship. I was beyond excited, as going to Europe and traveling was a dream of mine.

The relationship with the man I loved was rocky but now that he had admitted he loved me back, things became easier. I was more assured and when I heard from him I felt fulfilled. He had explained his fears and that he wished he had the courage to tell me he loved me when I said it to him many months prior. He was still working on ships as I left for my Europe trip. I was curious to see if we could meet up when I was near where he was porting, or if maybe I could go cruise with him after my trip.

The trip to Europe was exactly what I wanted. It gave me the confidence I needed to explore another country on my own and I did the trip my way. I respected my needs. The other people on the trip with me were very interested in drinking and partying. I was interested in food and sightseeing. The culture of the places I was visiting was important for me to experience. I was spending only a few days in each place and wanted to know if I wanted to return to any of the places I visited. I wish everyone could travel in their twenties to experience other countries, and see that people have many different ways of living.

Returning home from Europe, I planned to go visit my love for a week. He had quit the ship and wanted to go back to school. Then I would go on my third contract which would provide new challenges. I was excited to go see him. We spent a week in his hometown together. Meeting his mom was the first time I was meeting a lover's mom. At the time we were not exclusive, but he loved me, and I loved him. We felt like we were in a relationship even though we were not. After the trip, it became clear to me that he had definitely been with other women. He had passed on an STI to me, and what's worse—he didn't feel anything about it; he didn't apologize for not getting tested or the fact that it caused me physical pain. I felt so insignificant to him, like he didn't care if I lived or died or was healthy or not. Although I knew he loved me, I was not secure enough at the time and did not truly know how having proof that he had been with other women and didn't care how this STI might have affected us. He didn't go to a clinic to get tested; he just listened to me be upset. Looking back, I wanted him to not feel the need to be with others because I wanted to be enough for him—whatever that means. I wanted him to feel anything about giving me an STI; I wanted to know I mattered to him.

What is enough? We talk about it all the time in society, this unobtainable level that we need love to reach. Enough is unquantifiable. I felt like I wasn't enough to stop my mom from committing suicide and now I felt like I wasn't enough for a man I loved, to be his only sexual partner. This notion comes from society and the pressure we put on each other to be enough for someone other than ourselves—enough that we will go against what we might need or want for the other person. Monogamy is pounded into our heads, which at the time I didn't need from him, but I did need him to be responsible and realize that he was putting me at risk. Violating our own self respect is one thing but he violated me. Yet, if I love and accept someone for who they are, then why would I ever need or ask them to disrespect themselves for me? He unfortunately didn't ask me before he disrespected me and my body. I didn't know at the time this was how I felt. I had forgiven him immediately for giving me an STI and was thankful it wasn't deadly and I got treated. However, I felt betrayed—first by him for not getting tested, and second by myself. I trusted him and we hadn't used a condom. I allowed this and that was something then I had to take responsibility for, and now accept. The above realization was and still is maddening. It goes back to the concept of questioning whether at one point your self-respect overrides the respect you hold for other humans. Where is the line and how easy is it to hop from one side to the other on the priority list of respect? Do you have to sacrifice your respect for others if you are going to give your own self respect power?

13. We were on a Break

Three weeks into rehearsals for my next contract I was cutting an avocado and the knife slipped, went through the avocado, and into my hand. Thankfully, it didn't hit anything major, but my ego was majorly bruised, and I was in Tampa where I didn't have family and my lover couldn't be reached. I was alone. I felt so alone. Now and even then I wonder if this was truly an accident, if I was being stupid, or if I saw this happening and just didn't stop it. I remember thinking it was my fault because I was tired, but accidents happen.

The worst part is because I felt so alone, I started hating him. I wanted to push him away. I wanted to prepare for what he had told me would always be the truth—that he wasn't good enough for me and could never love me the way I ought to be loved. What's worse is he couldn't let me love him the way I wanted to love him. He constantly disrespected my need to just love him. I didn't want to hate him though. I wanted to love him, and not hurt him. I wanted to just love him and keep his heart safe. He wasn't there for me though, when I needed him. My thoughts obviously went wild and I knew I could hurt him too. I decided I had to try to move on like he told me I should. I had to try, he told me to, and I needed to protect myself. I remember making this choice; it broke my heart in a lot of ways, but I didn't want to hate him. Looking back I felt forced to make this choice.

We took a break. I know we are like Season Three Ross and Rachel from *Friends*. At the time, I was about to go on my third ship and I knew if I didn't try to get over him then I might be stuck yearning for him forever. Both of us deserved better. Both of us loved each other at this point. I wrote him a long email stating that I needed a communication break. I stated that I would still be around if he needed me but that I needed to see what life was with me trying to move on.

Safe to say that didn't work. A week after we started our break I had to get my appendix removed. I remember emailing him or calling him to tell him I was having surgery and all I wanted was for him to come fly to me; I was reaching through the phone but the words to ask just couldn't come out. I knew he wouldn't. He didn't. Although, to this day, I wish he had. All I wanted was to love him, to be near him, and to have him near me. All I wanted was for him to feel worthy of my love, and show up for me.

My sister flew out to get me out of the hospital and I knew I was taken care of; she made sure I knew I was taken care of. My sister is the best. Others did offer to come take care of me, including my step-mom. My sister was the right choice. She made me walk and we got ice cream.

Going on to my third contract on board ships a month later than intended because of my appendix, I felt behind. When I got on ship there were pay issues and the cast was unhappy. Ever since I had stabbed myself, I felt further and further behind—like there was a ladder extending above my head and no matter how much I climbed, I could not reach the top. I had let myself down in so many ways. I kept my chin up and pressed on.

At every turn I was letting myself down. I wasn't adjusting to this ship like the others, and now I didn't have my love to fall back on. I had started slipping into a depression that was dark and lonely. I remember feeling broken but unwilling to admit it to myself. It was like I had lost the ability to choose the right course, I was missing information and nothing I did was right. Finally, one of the technicians took me aside and confronted me about quite a few issues he was having with our tech supervisor. I had no idea what had been happening and quickly sprang into action to fix the issues. It was almost like a storm had been brewing since I stabbed my hand and everything had lined up properly to lead to these moments. If the feeling of being broken hadn't happened, I am not sure I would have seen that sometimes things really are out of our control. Sometimes the reason you feel like you can't stop the climbing ladder extending is because you don't have all the information. Maybe it is climbing to get you to a different world way above where you are now, and it's just making sure you are safe.

The upper management, not knowing the whole story, decided to remove me from the situation and bring me back to the rehearsal spaces in Tampa before sending me to a different ship. As I was leaving, I learned that the cast I had been working with was trying to get the Cruise Director fired and a lot of other ridiculous gossip. Looking back, I am beyond happy I was removed from that ship and from that situation. In the beginning I may not have been doing my best, but by the end I was—by the end I had made vast adjustments. By the end I had also reached back out to my love and told him that no amount of silence was going to change my love for him. The break did not work. I was still very much in love with him.

What happened next was something I never expected. I went on to another ship and gained my work confidence back. I made one friend on this last ship; I worked on and remember sending a letter, hand-written to my love explaining everything. Hoping he would respond and forgive me. I was being naïve again. Instead of forgiving me, he told me to leave him alone—to get out of his life.

He broke my heart. I always knew this was possible—that when I took a break from him it was possible I was doing irreparable harm to our relationship—but love conquers all, or so I thought. Love can heal all wounds and I loved him to the

best of my ability. Him telling me to leave him
alone was a slap in the face; it was like he was
saying get out of my life. "I don't want or need you
and won't have you be someone that is in my life."
It felt like my mother abandoning me all over again.

This realization took years for me to
understand. He gave me no explanation, like I had
given him; he simply said leave me alone. He didn't
tell me he'd always be there for me; he simply said
get out—I never want you in my life again. In some
ways I look back at this moment as a turning point
for me and him. He was giving up on me, and
himself, and I felt that. I thought I felt that. It was
the push—the betrayal I needed—to fall out of
being in love with him. To stop pursuing him. It
was the final show of how much he did not respect
me for me. How dare he not explain and abandon
me like that when he had told me he would always
be there for me?

The anger I had was changing. It was the
turning point in making the choice to fall out of love
with him. It strengthened my Mental Armor though.
It felt like he hadn't been honest with me that he
would always love me. I realized our definitions of
love were very different. He had told me to move
on and this was it, and this was what showed me I
needed to move on. I felt betrayed. I felt abandoned,
and he had told me he knew these feelings. He
hadn't treated me with understanding; he didn't
give me respect, but reacted with anger and fear.

Responsibility in hurt was not his alone. I knew I had hurt him when I asked for a break from him. He had left me no choice. He didn't show up for me—not just once but enough that it broke my heart. He caused me pain constantly by telling me I was dumb for loving him. How disrespectful to himself, and to me. I chose to love him. I chose to trust him with my heart. If he would have done his best to love me as much as he could have, then that would have been enough for him to be enough for me. Instead he told me to leave.

Walking off my last ship I had decided to move on. I knew it would take time. After almost two and a half years of being in love with this man it took me six months to figure out I was not longer in love with him. It required me to see him, and just know the love had changed. There was certainly love still present but I would no longer trust my heart in his hands until he showed me that he trusted me. I would no longer trust my balloon to be guarded by him.

13. *The Hardest Thing to Do*

December had just hit in 2016 and I was working for a prominent institution at the time. I had just gotten comfortable with not hearing from the man I used to be in love with. Getting an email from him made my heart stop. Fear set in. I was terrified when I read that he was coming to visit because I knew that my feelings had changed and I didn't want him in the same way as I once did. At the time, I felt so sure that I needed to see him because I thought that maybe if he saw me and told me everything, and took responsibility for himself, that maybe I would feel different.

Upon receiving that email, here is the list of fears I wrote in a journal on 12/17/2016:
No knowing what to say
Not being what he expects
Feeling different than I want to (I don't know if I knew how I wanted to feel)
Hating him
Don't want to make him hurt
Him or me hurting me
Not saying how I feel
Not being myself
Him disappointing me
Being let down
Feeling abandoned once again
Worrying about you hurting you

Agreeing to meet him for lunch was good. I remember setting my eyes on him and being a little nervous. We went to lunch and it didn't take long for me to ask him, "Why are you here?"

He answered that he was visiting a friend, whom he was staying with, and decided to ask me to catch up. I remember thinking, "He's lying. I don't know why but he is and I don't care. I don't want to call him on it, because I don't want to fight for him and I don't want to pull his teeth for the truth. If he isn't going to trust me with the truth, then he isn't worth my effort to fight to get him to be honest with me." I knew right then for sure I wasn't in love with him anymore. I knew I didn't want to waste my time trying to convince him to let me love him.

The suspicion had been there for a while but now I, without a doubt, knew I was no longer in love with him. I did, however accept him for whom he was and I still loved parts of him. Respect was always present on my end for him. I only ever loved him. Someone who couldn't tell me how much he loved me; someone who is so scared of abandonment that he doesn't give himself easy to someone else out of the fear. I saw that he didn't trust me, but I still wanted to care for him. I wanted to be there for him like I had always told him I would. I wanted him to fight for me and he just

didn't seem to want me enough to tell me the truth.
I needed to respect that; I had to talk myself into
this, but of course I wanted to ask why he was
lying.

Telling him I was no longer in love with him
was the hardest thing to do, but he had a right to
know where my feelings were. He had a right to
know I loved him but I would no longer
compromise myself for him because he didn't trust
me. Looking back I don't know if he was truly
listening to me after I told him I fell out of being in
love with him. I had taken my heart out of his
hands, even if I still cared for him. He was hurt by
me telling him I was no longer in love with him. I
know this because when he left, he sent me an email
shortly afterward saying he had sent me a letter.
Looking back, this seems so dramatic.

Reading the words he sent me, I saw that he
was brave in the end and I appreciated it so much,
but it was too little too late and it came with strings.
He professed his love for me. He told me he wanted
to give me everything I have ever wanted and yet
made me put a time limit on it, which meant he
didn't trust me. It took me a bit to realize this—to
realize how disrespectful that was to him and
myself.

We had a few visits after I received his letter
of love. I felt special, I felt like his exception. I felt
like this was my fantasy and yet I couldn't just
forget what lead us to this point. The in-love nature

was gone; I didn't want him in the same way. I felt like if I did something that he deemed as not ok, maybe he would go back to how he was. If he couldn't trust that I was going to really consider being in a relationship with him, I needed as much time as I needed to work through my anger for him and then he couldn't trust me long term. He couldn't respect himself or me enough to understand forgiveness takes time. I also needed to sleep with him again. Physical connection is and was important to me, and I wasn't sure if I could have an orgasm with a man that I felt betrayed by and that angered me to no end, and had hurt me the way he had. I had to find out in order to make a decision like this—to possibly fall in love with him again. I needed to have as much information as possible at each step I took with him, and I needed him to respect my time and know that I could not feel pressured.

Our last visit was at his home. It was a week around my birthday in 2017. I was twenty-seven and much different than the twenty-four-year-old that fell in love with him three years ago. That trip was amazing. I did sleep with him and I remember being emotional about it. I remember realizing that I could still have the sexual chemistry and relationship with him and it was all the more confusing because I hoped that the sexual connection would not be there and that would be it—that its lack would make up my mind for me. Instead I felt more connected to him than ever when I left his hometown.

Unfortunately, he didn't feel the same way.
Our having sex felt like a goodbye for him, and that
meant he was now afraid I was going to say
goodbye to him. The doubt he had in whether I
would drag out the decision to be with him hurt in
ways I still can't quantify. I was so hurt that he
didn't trust me. I only made the decision when I
was ready to make it, and I felt pressure to put a
decision date on it. I felt pressured to make this
choice that went against everything that I felt I
needed in a relationship. I felt trapped between what
he wanted me to do; I felt forced to choose between
him over me. I was worried I would always feel he
didn't trust me. When I asked why he needed a
decision date, his reasons all melted into four words
"I don't trust you" is what I kept hearing.

A family member of mine was the most
influential piece of the decision to not enter back
into a committed relationship with this man. Take
into account the only time we were committed to
each other was when we were on ship for the last
six weeks or so, but now I was trying to decide if I
wanted to be in a committed relationship with this
man in a matter of six months. There was so much
water under the bridge. Sex couldn't help; only time
could help. I had to really come to terms with my
realities and figure it out, so I turned to my family
for advice.

The problem is at this point was that I
already knew people have different definitions of

love. I wanted the opinion of someone who had been in love and then out of love and found their way back. My step-sister was the only person I knew who had really stuck it out in the way I felt most closely resembled my love story to this man, and even that was a stretch because the details were different and we are all entirely different people. I was looking for as many differing perspectives and views as I could get. I wanted stories so I could have a realistic picture of my own experience—a realistic vision of what my choice meant in the long run.

Something she said definitely stuck in my brain like a seed, and that was when she told me to look ahead in my life. I know who this man is, I know what struggles we've had, and I know that people fight about the same things over and over and over again. That's when it clicked. I did not want to be having these fights for the rest of my life or right now and he doesn't trust me. I don't want to be constantly trying to prove my loyalty. I do not want to be fighting to hear how much someone cares about me. I do not want feelings withheld from me, leaving me with only part of the information. I do not want to feel like the strong one in a relationship that has to point out that there is no trust in our emotional relationship. Values: I had to lay out my values and determine if he fits my values. The top value is honesty, and I felt like he struggled with his honesty which left me without vital information. This led us to a place of no trust

and a lack of respect on both sides. Values were
now plainly misaligned.

14. Values

The decision to not enter back into a relationship with a man I was so deeply in love with at one point was, as I stated, the hardest decision of my life. In addition to the decision to never try to commit suicide. I say this with an air of comedy, because for my entire life I wanted to be someone's choice; I wanted someone to choose me to love and to say I was enough. Now that someone had, and I had realized there is more to being in love than just loving someone, I wanted to dive into my needs more and fully dissect my values and standards. I had unlocked a new level to my standards, and having to convince someone that I was who I said I was was not something I thought was respectful, and I would have felt dishonest if I had handled the situation any differently. Yet, I knew I would always love him and respect him. I just could not put his needs above my own. I needed as much time as it took for me to forgive him, and he took that as me abandoning him.

Taking a hard look at yourself is no easy task but after breaking the heart of someone you thought you would marry, have babies with, and be in love with forever, I wanted to really break down what makes up my choice pattern and to determine whether my love for myself is real or whether it was something I was faking until I really gained the confidence.

Honesty became my top value. This was largely due to feeling so betrayed by my lover. He had kept information about his feelings to himself. Courage and trust are tied to honesty. Respect was next. Respect is the foundation of honesty and love. As I have said this wasn't clearly defined for me at the time, and after the relationship I realized how disrespectful it was. He was trying to protect me from him instead of simply showing me who he was and trusting that I can make my own choices of what I want for my life. Up until the last moments of our relationship he didn't understand respect in the way that I did. It isn't his fault in a way. I don't know if he viewed our relationship the same as I now see it, because two years later he is a ghost in my life. He could not see that I never wanted him out of my life; I just wanted him to respect me and believe I would respect him. Our communication was not sufficient during any part of our relationship.

Now I email him when I want, when I miss him. I always told him I would always be there for him and that I would always email him to tell him how I felt. When he said the same, it is now obvious to me that he either didn't mean it, or he didn't know what love and accepting someone for who they are really means. If he would have allowed me to get past my anger and hurt for him because of how he treated me and disrespected me, in my own time, I would have probably been engaged, or even married with kids right now. When I do think of him, I believe that I don't always have the right presumptions. It was the right thing for us to not get into a committed relationship when he asked. I would have cheated on him, and there would be no coming back from that. I knew it when I said I had to choose me. I knew I wouldn't have been able to not hurt him intentionally because I was angry that he didn't trust me. Disrespect is a deal breaker. Respect is of the upmost importance, and integral for a relationship to work.

Intelligence is another high value. I am thankful all the time that I had the emotional and social intelligence within me to know I could not get into a relationship with this man. That I would be compromising myself. There were times I had done this with him, and he had crushed my heart. I did not want to feel like the man I love is questioning my loyalty or my ability to know I want to be with him, and when he put a time limit on my decision because he needed it, it made me sick to know he didn't trust me to choose him.

Consistency, and I mean true consistency across all levels, is high on my values list. Consistency was something I lacked greatly growing up. Consistency is another word for integrity. I realized the lack of consistency that I had growing up is what ultimately made me feel unsafe. Only as an adult did I understand what feeling safe in an environment or with a person really felt like. Saying one thing and doing

something different or not saying you don't know
promotes false information.

As an example, when you tell someone you
will be somewhere at 6 p.m. and then something
happens, but you wait until the last moment to tell
the other person, you are disrespecting their time.
Mistakes happen; emergencies happen. However,
when a person says one thing and does something
different, for those who have experienced trauma,
the uncertainty of what is true or false can be
triggering of mental illness. The trust is shaken
when consistency fails.

I found that when a person is consistent with
me, communicates with me, and does what they say
they will do, it makes me feel safe in that
relationship. It makes me worry and fixate less on
the possibility that the person will choose to leave
me with no explanation like my mother did. It
makes me feel safe to share my feelings and not
worry if I disrespect them, because they don't react
out of fear, anger or hurt. Instead, the people I want
in my life are those that respond with love, respect,
kindness, and understanding.

Having drive is of high value to me. When I
come across people who don't have passions or
want happiness for themselves, it makes me
question whether they have self respect. Those that
have high self respecting values in terms of passions
or goals and are pursuing them attract me. Let me
break this down in a way that I have always looked

at my own life and those around me with realistic expectations: On any given day I live my life at a solid 7-8, sometimes I live at a constant 10, meaning I am happy. There are certain things that affect my happiness in either positive or negative manners, and drive comes in when the effects are negative. I will work hard to get my life to a place above a 6, preferably as close to 10 as possible. There are other people out there who find happiness in mediocrity; they need to have things to complain about and fixate on in order to have some type of control, or if their life drops below a certain standard they will work just hard enough to get their life back to mediocrity. I try to live above a mediocre life. I try to elevate my experience with people who enjoy conversations and fun in similar ways as my own wants and needs. I live my life to gain happiness and a sense of usefulness. Purpose and drive in others is and has always been important to me when it comes to my closest relationships.

These were all part of the decision. These all affected my choice to not say yes to everything I thought I wanted. I grieved for what was, and for the hurt that I had suffered by my own hand and his. I felt loss and responsible for his pain and my own. I was about to start an interesting point in my life where I would learn even more about myself and the world. I was about to be a Flight Attendant and I was excited for the adventure to come. I would be broken again. This time not at my own lack of abilities but by the thought that good prevails and

people care about people more than money. I was
wrong.

15. Into the Tin Can

April 2017 I started training to become a flight attendant. I was in a class with roughly twenty other adults. I had not been a flight attendant before but I had worked on ships which had a similar safety culture. I knew I was going to rock this course. I'm a good student and I speak my mind. I also learn quickly. Going into this new adventure I had so much excitement.

The optimism I had going into class was quickly diminished. The other people didn't like my confidence. They didn't like that I asked questions. They didn't like my outspoken nature. I know this because they told me. Looking back, I get it; sometimes people don't like confidence shoved in their face and I didn't apologize for my nature, or being myself. I adjusted. I rephrased some of my questions. I tried to be just a bit less to let others shine. This didn't change once I got on the aircrafts which would earn a special place in my heart.

While working on airplanes I was in a minority. In the company I worked for there weren't many white female confident women that are outspoken and not afraid to voice their opinions. One of the kindest co-workers I had while working for the airline was a woman who worked in international development prior—specifically in emotional intelligence. One day, after we had worked together at least a couple times, we were eating and I had heard her evaluate others. She was a master at holding a mirror up to others, and I admired her for this. It was intoxicating to be around someone so interested in people and so willing to see them. I was curious what she thought about me. I wanted her opinion because I valued it; she had shown me she had a beautiful power of observation and was kind and self aware in a similar way to myself. I remember her answer so vividly: she said, "You rub people the wrong way because you have the confidence of a colored woman, but you are white." I had never felt so seen by someone who didn't know me all that intimately. She went on to say I am very self-aware and have a true want to be kind and helpful, but sometimes people get rubbed the wrong way by me because they mistake my confidence for entitlement, and they mistake my excitement to be heard for disrespect. People don't know how to handle my enthusiasm because it's rare. I had to do better at adjusting, but how to do this without making myself small? How do I work in tight quarters with people who are insecure with themselves and decide to not like me for their insecurities? How do I not feel so alone, when everyone seems to be putting me in a box?

Focus on the good people. Flying, and being a flight attendant has brought me my best friend. A woman I call my soul mate. That being said, I know that in order for her to be in my life for as long as I

would like, it is a choice we both constantly make.
As someone with abandonment struggles I worry
about the amount of love I have for her. However,
every day that she is in my life I am thankful for my
time as a flight attendant in bringing her into my
world. The people I met while flying were some of
the best people I had ever met. It is not a job for
people with too many insecurities.

Flying and being a flight attendant taught
me more about myself than any other job has ever
taught me. Having to handle the many differing
personalities and how different views on the world
can open your eyes to other ways people get
through the struggles was empowering, and
saddening. Flying as a flight attendant was an
immensely positive and negative experience for me,
and I consider myself lucky to have had the
experience for as long as I did.

Here is a blog post I made on September 4, 2017:

Talking to Strangers

Recently, I read a post about the ironic situation
created when men tell women as they are growing
up not to talk to strangers and then get upset when
an attractive woman doesn't talk to them. I thought
it to be quite funny.

I on the other hand was encouraged to talk to
strangers growing up. My parents jokingly would

say, "Don't talk to strangers," but everywhere they went would then strike up conversations with random people and I am thankful for that. I wish they had explained that some strangers were tricksters and to be careful of what strangers I talk to because not everyone is kind. I now see there may have been some mixed messages in what they said verses what they did.

Throughout my career, both in theater and now in aviation, the ability to talk to anyone has been an asset.

On my last flight, I struck up a conversation with an older gentleman. He was older, born in 1941, but I'm guessing by the conversation we had (that led me to find out when he was born), that he would not want to be called older. However, I did explain that I consider age and being older to be a badge of honor and a thing to be celebrated. It will be gift one day to be called old by, if all goes well, grandchildren or other children.

Back to the man; he is a film and book writer. We talked for maybe a half hour about NYC and a book he wrote that he wants to turn into a musical movie because a musical would be too expensive, which prompted a response from me because I know the theater world.

It was a wonderful exchange and a much needed distraction during a slightly annoying flight.

Right there, at the end, I clearly knew I was having an annoying flight. I chose to write about the good. This man who didn't have to talk to me and tell me his story chose to take the time. The job taught me to be patient with myself, most of all. For that I am thankful for the job, but it also broke me in a way that would be quite traumatic if it weren't for the fact that I hadn't dealt with other traumas first.

My feelings about flying would soon change. At a time when I was thinking about upgrading to be a senior cabin crew member I found myself having to stick up for myself morally and ethically to the airline I worked for and to try to make them see that they were promoting a culture of silence and unsafe practices that could lead to lives being lost.

16. Naïve and Broken

September 2018 was about to be a month to remember. Growing up, you watch movies or hear about how corrupt people are and how money can make people evil. The idea that corporations are out for money and don't care about human cost or life is drummed into you and yet, I always wanted to believe in the good in people. I've gotten my heart broken a lot by being intentionally naïve to the evil or malicious motives that everyone warns you about, and yet I prefer to keep operating by believing in others' kindness and positive intentions because I would rather be an optimist. I realize that this optimism is blinding and maybe I need to see more clearly; I need to have a healthy balance of optimism and realism, and then my social ideologies can take it from there. It gets increasingly harder to be an optimist when incidents like the fallowing occur:

Blog post from January 21, 2019 about 4 months after the initial incident:

Unfit to Fly

Corporations are huge. To stand up to them is a great undertaking.

Let me set the scene:

A crew of eight leaves delayed out of NYC heading to a far away land. We get in later than expected after working almost five hours more than expected.

The aircraft, which happens to be the main reason for the delay, is the same aircraft we will be going back to NYC on the following evening.

The next day after very little rest because of a broken shade in my room, I was notified of another delay on our flight back home—three hours later, which pushes us into a later night shift of work.

We arrive at the airport. The plane hasn't even landed. It's another forty-five minutes to an hour before the plane is at the gate. We board and are told there is a technical issue and we won't be going anywhere for a bit. We have no idea if a bit is an hour or five.

Then we are told the pilots will time out. Then, that there is a solution in place for that problem. Then, that the plane problem isn't solved.

Then we are told that the plane isn't going anywhere.

At this point it is four and half hours on the plane. We get to the five-hour mark of having been on the plane and are told we can now leave and boarding will start in twenty minutes.

The crew is wrecked; we are exhausted. The whole situation was mismanaged. We try to discuss our lack of fitness to fly but are bullied into not thinking we can choose to be safe. We spring into action trying to figure out how to make rest work and augmented service because of the extra time and regulations and we were at minimum crew but the passengers needed to eat.

Then all of the sudden we remember that speaking up and saying that we are not fit to fly is an acceptable option—or so we think and have been taught in training. When we do speak up and just start the conversation about our fitness to work, the captain mistakenly pressures us to work. We are unfit though and to have gone would have been a mistake. To have left in our state would have been a safety issue.

Safety is important. That's the official company line. If that were truly the case, you would not suspend your workers for doing what they think is right and admitting to not being in the right mind to hold people's lives in their hands.

■ ■

I was part of an eight-person crew that night, when we individually decided to call Not Fit to Fly in to the flight operations. This ultimately cancelled our flight, resulted in an investigation, disciplinary action, and was a contributing factor to my firing from the company.

After the night we called in Not Fit To Fly, we went through a few traumatic dealings because of the incident. I didn't realize quite how traumatic that actual night was for a bit of time and it was only traumatic because the company showed us little support and little regard. I can honestly say looking back: I know I did the right thing. When every choice came up, I would not have chosen any path differently. I chose the path that prevented harm to myself that could have resulted in anyone's loss of life. I chose keeping everyone alive.

What happened is described as a rolling delay. Our captain should have handled the situation better. At the end of the day they punished us, the flight attendants, when **I believe the responsibility lies with the corporation and the culture of silence, fear, and false integrity.**

Our captain was new to the company. He said while chastising us for speaking up about our exhaust, that if we called in Not Fit To Fly there could be repercussions or punishment. At the time I remember being outraged that he didn't have more loyalty to the company or to us—or to humankind. We were trying to state that we didn't feel safe and he was pressuring us to leave out of fear that he might be punished. I couldn't describe this then because I was being naïve. He was right, and this realization that this company didn't care about a human life but instead they cared about money, only happened after everything unfolded.

There is no doubt in my mind that if we would have left, if anything–and I mean anything— would have happened that was abnormal, I don't think I would have been of any use. This could have been a medical emergency, or a fire, or a rude passenger. I now realize how lucky I am that I decided to listen to my body and mind telling me that I could not handle any emergency and therefore was unfit to perform my safety duties, meaning I could have been saving someone's life by simply being self aware. If anyone had a heart attack in front of me, I would have been devastated beyond consoling if they had died because of my lack of abilities under the conditions. I was unfit.

The company then showed its true colors. I was kept stranded for the next three days—two days longer than my fellow colleagues—and then worked the flight home, to where I landed to an email stating I was suspended. I burst into tears. This was the first time I ever went to a bar to get drunk because of my emotions. The shots slid down like candy and I openly cried at a bar that I frequented. I was devastated. I was shocked, I was sad, and I was angry. I felt so disrespected by the company that I wanted to feel nothing.

The captain was right. This company is going to punish us, they are going to discipline us, and they don't see how they are putting people's lives at stake. They don't see that suspending us with base pay is a punishment, because almost 30-40% of our pay comes from per diems and extra hours. They don't see that when you suspend us, even with base pay, you are taking money out of our pockets that we rely on and are removing us from society. They set meetings with each of us—or started to then, stopped because the head offices said they needed to investigate. Which now made us all worry, except me. I got very suspicious that they were going to fire us but someone intervened and now they were trying to cover their asses by doing an investigation. It felt deliberate and chaotic because this situation had never happened before, or so they said. They had never had an entire crew call in Not Fit To Fly. They didn't have a union to mitigate this, and there wasn't anything we actually did wrong.

Recording my investigation interview was a no brainer. NYC is a one-party consent state, meaning if I am present and contribute even in the smallest way to a conversation, I can be the one party to consent to a recording. I went in there with my guard up. They had fired one of my colleagues the first week after we returned home for a bogus social media post. However, I understand that what she did violated their social media clause. We never discussed her firing in detail, but as far as I knew, that was her only issue. I had been informed already by my fellow crew that the questions being asked were specifically geared toward trying to find someone to admit that one person convinced others to call in to intentionally make a point. I am the wrong one though to test. I don't do anything to go along with a crowd. I know my limitations and when I am ok and when work is too much. I trust myself. I am confident in my body's responses to stress and anxiety because I have tested myself in those regards. I have a wicked memory and I don't do anything because someone else is doing it. We followed the rules and our senior cabin chief knew what was happening and the captain was told by one of the cabin crew; we did it by the book they taught us. I was confident in my choices.

Catching them in their lies happened a few times in my interview. The first one was that they said they removed us from society because they wanted to make sure we were ok. I said, "That is a lie, because if that were true, if you really cared, then I wouldn't have worked home the night of the suspension. You would have pulled me off that flight and sent me home passive. I worked." They replied, "I didn't know that." I said, "I told you I worked home so that's a lie too, and I have the texts to prove it." I said everything I wanted to say. I stuck up for my colleagues and I stuck up for myself. When asked if I felt my work environment promotes a safe culture, I said, "No, I don't because of investigations like this. I did until this happened. You can conduct an investigation without taking our flight hours or my entitled day-off pay from the second day operations kept me from base. When you take punitive action against something in place for safety and our education and say to us that it isn't meant to not be punitive but then is, you promote a culture of silence and fear to speak up when something isn't safe." They put all of us on final warnings, demoted our senior, and one girl got fired for posting satire on social media. We were punished.

Going back to work was hard now. I felt betrayed and beaten and mentally abused. When a trip to that same city came up and I experienced another rolling delay (thankfully not as bad but similar), I got anxious and slightly emotional. I told my senior about this and thankfully it was handled much better, but I knew enough to know the nerves are important to talk about. It didn't impair my judgment but made me more vigilant. I was hyper-aware of my feelings. I'm still working through the trauma.

Four weeks go by and I get another trip, only it's longer—five days—and the last night was to the city that I now felt was just bad luck. I didn't realize this until the first leg of the trip and it hit me. I am going back there. The last two times I was there something bad happened, is this going to be three out of three.

Here is a description of everything that ensued after this realization from my blog:

Abuse of Power

Bullying is a form of harassment where someone uses their position of power to intimidate, shame, or lessen you. The power part is important, and it can be power physically, or emotionally, or professionally or in any number of scenarios.

I recently had an experience where it was clear that I couldn't just sit back and allow it to occur. I'll tell my side.

First leg of the trip: I was speaking with a fellow cabin crewmember about an incident I was involved in previously (this is above, Unfit to Fly), after the crew member asked me about it. It got me slightly emotional (just shy of tears) and instead of staying with the crew member, I went to discuss my worries with the senior. We had been taught to lean on our senior cabin crew. I thought this man was my friend as well; he had been helpful in the past.

After telling the senior, I was relieved but the senior was not very empathetic and he wasn't very consoling. I basically had to defend myself further to him and convince him that I was ok after stating that I got emotional because of two specific similar situations where one was handled properly and the original was not, but that it felt like the city on the last leg of this trip was causing me bad luck. He should have reassured me that everything would be fine instead of admonishing me for being emotional.

Then when we arrived at the hotel, the senior pulled me aside and told me our conversation was troubling to him. He also shamed me for having emotions. Verbatim, he said there should be "no crying while flying." He told me he had never had any drama like this on his flights and I was confused because as far as I was concerned it was a good flight. I did everything required of me safety-speaking and in terms of service. I asked him to elaborate on what drama he was talking about and he said I was continually talking about a past incident and I shouldn't be. This was confusing because we were taught to promote safety and when people asked me about the event I felt obligated to tell them what happened to dispel rumors. I was there after all. It was my own experience to share.

I exclaimed that I was directly involved in this incident which others have approached me about and has to do with safety, so I have a right and an obligation to dispel rumors and talk to my colleagues about the incident to better inform them. I found this entire exchange very concerning because not only did I feel misunderstood, but also shamed for having feelings and singled out for no apparent reason. During this time, the senior also told me he was debating writing me up and as I am on a final warning (he knows this because his roommate was involved in the same incident which placed me on final warning). He didn't want to report me as it could cause me to be fired. He also stated that tomorrow is a new day and he hopes no other drama will occur.

The next leg of the trip was a great flight. A colleague who is a senior but not the senior on this trip (flying low rank) made fun of me (at the time I thought it was in good fun as I get along with this colleague) and mentioned that I wasn't wearing lipstick. She had mentioned this on the previous flight. In both instances I was wearing lip gloss or lip balm. Our manual is ambiguous about lip make-up and doesn't clearly state what is required. To please this colleague, I put on a bright red lipstick. It was meant as a joke but looking back I felt embarrassed that she was making such a big deal about it.

She then continued to point out my lipstick to the senior on the trip and asked him to clarify if lipstick was mandatory, pointing out that he was my boss. I pointed out the ambiguity in the manual and said I would text our base chief for clarification, which I did, and she said it is mandatory. I then apologized to both seniors if I had given them a hard time, not realizing how dehumanized I felt, or how admonished I felt.

The next day I showed up for the third leg of the trip. I had a nude lipstick on as I had misplaced the red lipstick and the only other colors I had were bright pink and dark brown. I also had a bag of food with me which was not regulation but depending on the senior sometimes they allow it. Our manuals state we can only carry luggage provided by the company, but they do not give us bags for food and therefore unless you purchase them, how am I supposed to bring food with me? This is why some seniors are more lenient with this rule. They understand and are human about food requirements.

When we arrived at the airport the senior approached me in front of the crew and verbatim said "Do you want to work this flight?" I said, "Yes".

He then criticized my lipstick saying it had shades of blue or black and it was unacceptable and then I motioned to the bag and asked if he'd like me to take the lipstick off and throw out the bag. He confirmed and then proceeded to lecture me and bully me. He used his seniority and his position of knowledge of my final warning to say he could have me fired.

I proceeded to throw out my purchased food and take my lipstick off. I then presented him with the colors of lipstick I had. He chose the dark pink color which sufficed.

As far as I know, I was not made aware of any other drama or issues with other crew members.

We got to our destination and I could feel that I was being talked about behind my back and was not being made aware of issues. I had, to the best of my ability, done everything the cabin chief had asked of me while other crew members were not held to the same standard.

I felt singled out and embarrassed.

When I got to the hotel I was informed by HR that a crew member had made a complaint and asked I be

removed from my flight the next day which was
supposed to be my line check.

I informed HR that I was sorry for the extra work I
may have caused them and I would be happy to
discuss the situation at length once home and if the
senior wants me removed I'd cooperate, as that is a
safety issue. I then phoned our operations staff to
see if they could send me home that same day as to
save the company money and not require them to
buy my day off as they could not send me home the
following day.

I feel like I was bullied and singled out
unnecessarily by the cabin chief. I also feel like this
incident was created by poor management and
while the cabin chief was blaming me for creating
drama, he was the one in fact either creating the
drama or allowing others to create it.

That's the whole of it. I submitted almost that same
accountancy in my report and will wait to see the
outcome. I am mostly disappointed in the situation
as a whole and tried my hardest to diffuse the
situations as they arose. I wish I had been more
successful.

■■■

About a full month later, the company fired me.

Currently, I am suing the company for
discrimination because they fired me partially for
not complying with a vague but mandatory
regulation to wear lipstick, where as men were not

allowed to wear make-up which means it was
discriminatory based on my sex to require and then
partially fire me for requiring something based on
sex.

When I was fired I was upset. I got
depressed. I could not believe that my final
warning, from standing up for what I thought was
moral and ethical, was a part of me being fired. I
felt humiliated and angry at the abuse of power and
couldn't understand how a company could do this to
an employee who would have been loyal to no end
and worked for many years for them. I was a bit
heartbroken. At the time, I didn't even have the
emotional capability to realize the discrimination
because I was caught up in the total disregard for a
human life—for kindness, for truth, and for moral
and ethical reasons I knew I needed to stand up for
myself. I wouldn't be able to look myself in the
mirror if I didn't. I felt discriminated against for
carrying about my own life and the life of others. I
felt labeled as having an inappropriate attitude. I felt
admonished for being the guard of my own safety
and then the safety of those the company had placed
under my responsibility.

Looking for a lawyer is never something I
thought I would have to do—especially because of a
job. I never wanted to feel so wronged or abused by
an employer that I would have to seek out a lawyer,
but this corporation managed to disrespect my life
so gravely and the lives of its patrons that I felt
obligated to do so, as others were too scared.

When I told other people I cared about what I was doing, the feedback I got was not what I expected. I remember feeling not supported and very lonely. I was embarrassed that people thought I was stupid and nothing would come of it. This realization brought me to tears. I didn't realize why people thought me seeking justice was so unattainable until March 2020, when CoVid – 19 broke out and it was made clear socially that capitalism operates from the top down, with the view that money is more important than human life when you live in the United States to the Government.

Later I wrote this letter to my lawyer regarding my lawsuit which dealt solely with the sexual discrimination, but tried to describe why the discrimination in my mind was still heavily connected to both the firing event and my calling in Not Fit To Fly:

I made a self-diagnosis of imposter syndrome. My working diagnosis from my therapist is adjustment disorder. I am going to talk to my therapist about my imposter syndrome diagnosis because it is so relative. It is kind of like a lie detector for when someone disrespects my humanity—my rights— which unfortunately are not always written in law in a way that is true.

Imposter syndrome is extreme feelings of inadequacy.

Adjustment disorder is extreme feelings when anything traumatic occurs.

The combination of these two means that I have extreme feelings of inadequacy when I feel like someone disrespects my human rights as I see them. Once I feel this disrespect I then jump into the adjustment-syndrome mode and go to an extreme with my emotions because being respected for who I am—my morals and ethics—is life or death for me because of my past, present, and future.

On the NFF, the pilot disrespected my right to state if I was able to safely perform my duty to hold my own and other's lives in my hand; therefore he triggered my imposter syndrome and discriminated against me for it, making me doubt my human right to keep myself alive. My own life felt at risk operating that flight, and the company then suspended me for trying to keep myself alive. I just took up "arms" by using my mind instead of any other means.

The company then triggered my adjustment syndrome by suspending me for standing up for my own human right to live and keep myself safe or bear arms against any one. I was just taking up "Arms with my mind, instead of any other means."

I don't know if you can follow my train of thought.

It is a Second Amendment issue, but instead of a gun to bear arms, I used my mind to bear arms.

They discriminated not just against me for lipstick
but for using my mind.
This is why I tie the two incidents together.

I find it fascinating and I will be discussing it with
my therapist but the Second Amendment states "A
well regulated militia, being necessary to security of
a free state, the right if the people to keep and bear
arms, shall not be infringed."

I was using my mind as a weapon or "Arms" to
rightfully keep people safe that are vital to the
security of my state. I was doing the same in the
entirety of the incident regarding lipstick.

I am still using the Second Amendment to go after
them, for putting the public in danger.

This feels big because it states that you can use your
mind as a weapon. If a person is not fully aware of
your motivations. If morals and ethics are not taught
to you properly. If you do not have respect for both
human life and death, then how can you know if
you are using a weapon properly? Your mind can be
very powerful.

Supporting other people is a very hard thing to do if
a person doesn't know what they need to feel safe. I
found my support in a lawyer's office, and just like
that I stood up for myself and became my own hero.
This was probably the first time in my life where I
was fully aware and conscious of why I was making
that choice. I was protecting my rights to live. I had

to say "I am my own hero" to myself over and over before walking into my lawyer's office and telling them my story. I felt entirely inadequate because people my entire life have been telling me this—maybe they didn't realize how much they were telling me, with words or actions—but I certainly was listening. Thankfully I also had examples of people who were strong and had the morals and ethics I now knew I possessed. My Mental Armor was clearly now aware that I was not inadequate but fully and unequivocally capable to make life or death choices. I am capable of change, and capable to hold my own life in my hands, and I choose to live out of respect for humankind.

17. I am my own HERO

Growing up there are all of these heroes we hear about—some are religious, like Jesus, and Moses, and others are societal, like Marvel and DC heroes. Others are the heroes we see in the news and some could say their heroes are famous people because they follow their dreams; our perception is that a hero is someone that can do or be anything because they are the anything we see. During CoVid-19 pandemic, all healthcare workers and people that had been not seen as heroes became vital to human life. They can be our saviors—not even in the religious sense, but in the sense of needing other humans to have different skills to work together for humanity's greater good.

At age twenty-nine about to be thirty, I can without a doubt say I am my own hero, and I don't plan to stop being that person for myself for the rest of my life. Finally, my self respect has shown me that I do not need to be a martyr unless I choose. It is not your responsibility to put others before yourself but to make yourself healthy so that you can help others and yourself. Everything you've read has led me to this point in my life where standing up for myself and finding my voice is no longer an option; it is as necessary as breathing. That doesn't mean I don't still struggle with depression, or feelings of inadequacy, or body image struggles, or insecurities, or abandonment fears, or lack of confidence in new situations. At thirty, a year ago I was jobless, as I am currently, and I was devastated. I didn't dwell on the inadequacy as much as I used to; I just kept moving forward. Every time I feel I am alone, I remember who has been there for me, including and most assuredly myself and the choice I have to choose life, while understanding that there have been times in the past when I wanted to die.

Turning twenty-nine was nothing special. Six weeks later I got a job I had always wanted, back in theater management. Up until getting this job I had been searching for a new career. I was tired of always searching for jobs in theater. The industry which once had been my way to help others was now cold, and it felt as though it had turned its back on me. It felt as though it was threatening my very life to try and keep working in it. I would get interview after interview and yet no job offers. The people interviewing me would give me positive feedback but then go with another candidate. I felt constantly like I was missing something, which fed my insecurities so greatly to an extreme level. I thought I was missing an easier career that could make me money enough to have a family and allow me to get my dreams.

Money. I'm pretty sure everyone has this opinion, but I hate and love money. The new job I took felt like the answer. I was going to be a finance assistant, finally. This job was the missing piece to me getting to a place where I could maybe make enough money to start my own family. It could provide me with skills that might lead to a place I could call my home in terms of a career. I had no idea what I was in for though.

Starting this job, I knew I needed to do my best in order to prove myself. After all, all you can do is do your best with the tools you have already gathered. That was my experience. To do my best. During the interview process my boss eerily reminded me of my step-mom. What I didn't realize was that this boss was going to be important in me realizing abusive behaviors from my childhood that I didn't know were abusive by literally giving me similar abuse.

For ten months I worked for this company. I learned my position as quickly as I could but quicker than expected, and my smarts and my ability were taken for granted and used against me. I started off strong; I proved I was smart. Then my boss had to have surgery and I dropped the ball a bit. People make mistakes. The reality is that I took on all the responsibility. I adjusted. Before my boss went in for surgery there were a few times I had discussed with her that she did not speak to me in a way that was constructive and was mean and abusive; I realize now that she was constantly disrespecting my own human nature. I asked her questions as best as I could, but when you are learning it's hard to ask a question about something you don't know because you don't know it. She and the head of the company admitted to not being good teachers. **I tried to not take too much responsibility but it was hard because my boss never took any responsibility.** She went off for her surgery having told me that things would change and that a lot of her attitude toward me was due to her physical pain.

When she returned I dropped the ball a bit. I was making mistakes and this was because the consistency in the company is non-existent and I was doing my best to go with the flow while she was out of office recovering. I decided to talk with the company owner and he brought up the items I had been dropping the ball with; it would have been nice if my boss would have been able to do this in a constructive and non-abusive way. I owned up to my shortcomings; he was not wrong. I had been making mistakes, however most of them were because I still had learning to do. I had lost a bit of focus and admitted to that. The environment was a contributing factor but it was me and my choice to focus; I needed to step it up. That is exactly what I did. Adjusting and adapting are qualities that are inherent in humans because of the choices we get to make. We can choose to change, but first we have to be unafraid of the change.

The discussion with the company owner happened in October of 2019. I started working for the company April 2019. My boss's surgery was July 2019, and during August and September we were understaffed. It was rough. Finally come end of October we started gaining personnel and our season started picking up. Things with my boss were worse than ever. I started documenting the issues, noting that she would ask for one thing, then change her mind, and then go back to the original. There was no consistency.

It was like I was given a question that had five answers: A, B, C, D, E, but each time the question came up the answer would change. This happened from the top down but in different ways. Another contributing factor was that the owner and my boss had often differing views on how they wanted things done. When I would ask which answer I was using today I would be met with anger and dissatisfaction that I couldn't do my job, which was damaging to my already existing inadequacy. I couldn't read their minds and was then met with admonishment over my logic to ask questions. There is no book of logic that is universal, because humans are all different and respecting differences is not universal.

Where was my support? The job of a boss is to support your staff so they can support you and lead a company in a healthy productive way. It is just as much a two-way street as any communication. **I felt so unsupported and berated, demeaned, and degraded that my mental health had started to affect my physical health.**

Being that our country is in the middle of pandemic, this concept is most importantly relevant.

Having someone lead that knows how to support rather than demean and degrade is important to all of what makes a human, human. When you do not support properly, humans can choose, or unknowingly start to question their humanity.

My depression started to seep in after realizing how degraded and demeaned I felt. I couldn't make my boss happy at work and I take immense pride in my work. I was allowing this person to affect me in ways that made me upset because I was doing my job and yet I was being threatened at work almost every day unintentionally. I was experiencing PTSD from the discrimination at my previous job for standing up for myself. I was angry that I had been wrongfully fired and now had to suffer at a job I once thought would be a home for me to grow and flourish much like I thought at the airline would hopefully become. I had to mourn the prospect of staying in this job for longer because the thought of staying at this job was making me sick in all ways. I had to come to terms with the fact that I didn't have to just take the abuse. I had other choices.

Figuring out that I felt abused was its own journey. The woman who was my boss treated me similarly to the way I remember my step-mother treated me growing up. I like to use the dishwasher example.

Growing up my step-mom would get upset with me and my sisters for not helping with the dishes or putting dishes in the dishwasher. However, then when we would put them in the dishwasher we would get yelled at. There was never an explanation of why she was yelling at us and no matter what way we tried we would get yelled at. There was always something we were not doing right. Eventually, I started feeling trapped by inconsistency. I didn't know if I should help with the dishes or not, because no matter what, I would be yelled at. It was entrapping and it affected my self worth because oftentimes, my step mom would get angry and say mean things which made me feel bad about myself because I felt as though I was causing it—like I felt I caused my mother's death by not being enough to save her from committing suicide.

Let me be clear. My step-mom did the best she could. Later in life, she realized her standards are different than others' and that is a part of her limitations. Some of her standards cannot be met by others and she cannot expect others to meet them. She deals with this in her own way and I respect her for it. My step-mom assumes instead of presumes, **meaning she makes factual assumptions instead of presumptive observations, and she doesn't know when or how to asking the proper questions.** This is exactly the same with my previous boss. She is incapable of relinquishing control and doesn't have the communication capabilities to provide clear expectations or consistent practices, partially because the company owner struggles with consistency. When he controls my boss she feels the need to micro-manage and control others. It is a vicious and awful cycle. She wonders why no one lasts more than a year in the position I held. I chose to stop blaming her; I never treated anyone at this job with anything but respect. When people didn't do something right, instead of belittling them, I approached them with kindness and asked how I could better help them with their job, so I could do my own.

Quitting that job was one of the hardest things I have ever done. It was also one of the biggest life-saving things I ever did. The job made me grow a lot and it was the first steady, stable job I had ever had. When I started it, it had potential and I had to grieve that when I chose to lose the stability I was desperate to find. While I was at this job, I had also started my sexual exploration which was huge in me becoming the person always hoped I would be. It was the perfect storm for me to get %100 healthy, both in mind and in body.

18. Let's talk about Sex

On May 25, 2019, a month after I got the job I spoke about above, I went on a first date with a man I met on Tinder. I know this was the exact date because I got my cartilage pieced and like to keep track of my piercings as my body heals from them. Six weeks later I caught him and my roommate making out in the hallway of my apartment building. This was devastating to me. It felt like a betrayal that was so disrespectful to the person I had shown both of them I was, and it felt intentional, because they both told me they knew better.

The roommate was the only female roommate in my five-bedroom apartment other than myself. Up until this point we had discussed many personal items between us, and I thought she was a good person. I thought she respected me. I can honestly say that if they had come to me and said, "Hey we are attracted to each other. Would you be ok with us exploring each other in a romantic way?" I would have been very supportive of the exploration. My ego would have been bruised but I would have been supportive because I would have respected them; I would have encouraged them. I would have been proud to get out of their way and respect them because they would have been showing me respect.

Instead they chose to go behind my back and instigate drama and betrayal and majorly disrespect me. Being genuinely worried for a fellow woman's safety, which is traumatic considering my own history with disrespect, caused me to continually worry about my roommate's safety that then she continued to date this man. Disrespect can make you feel unsafe in your own home. What's worse is the fear I had when she left.

My experience with men is extensive and my roommate's was not. This guy that she made out with had just made a choice to disrespect me in no small way, which means he is capable of disrespecting her in large ways. Forever more, if they remain together that will always be how their relationship started, and I know from experience if a relationship starts with disrespect, then it will be the root of all the fights to come. I respect their decision. However, I also pity them.

We had not defined our relationship. He had told me however he loved me one night when drunk; he also mentioned I was too good for him. How right he was. He wasn't even decent to me the night the above disrespect happened, when I approached him to find out his reason for his actions. Instead of apologizing and saying there is no excuse, he not only didn't take responsibility but tried to tell me there was something wrong with me, that I caused this, and that it was my doing that he had a better connection with my roommate. How shitty to blame the woman that he now wanted to be in a relationship with for his choice to disrespect another human. This is why I will always see him as a threat to my friend. How disrespectful to me and to her. At this point I told him he could leave. He had crossed the line to tell me there was something wrong with me or that I had any bearing on his choice. I had been open and honest with him. I had told him how much honesty meant to me and he chose to go behind my back and then attack me for it instead of owning his decision to do something disrespectful. He was inherently disrespectful and couldn't take responsibility and in turn disrespected me and the woman that went on to become his girlfriend. He did me a favor. He showed me how disrespectful he truly was, and for that I am thankful. I hope he treats my roommate with more respect than me, she does deserve it. What's more is, for months he was around me and never apologized. He never took responsibility. My roommate did. She is amazing.

I pride myself on not releasing others' information but my roommate and I had some in-depth conversations about sex and each of our pasts. I knew who she was and I was worried for her when they kept seeing each other. I don't trust her judgment because she has given me a valid reason to not trust her judgment. However, I do respect her choices. As for him, I still think he is a disrespectful person and has the ability to seriously harm her. I hope he stays faithful to her, I hope they get married and have babies, and I hope he brings her all the happiness that she deserves. I was fixated for a long time on the anger I had toward him. I had never been betrayed like that before. Openly and when there was such a clear right choice, they both chose the wrong one. The difference is that she took responsibility for her choice and he did not.

This broke me. **I had to reclaim my sexual self**. Mostly because he had made me feel pressured to have sex with him in the first place. I was proud of three things. One: I didn't go down on him. Two: He wasn't very good at sex. Three: He said I love you and then said I deserved better, and he was right. I was hurt, but I had a right to be. They both chose to hurt me.

Starting my sexual exploration, I decided to do some research into the sex scene in NYC. I had been exposed to polyamorous relationships a few times in my life. The first time on cruise ships and then again while flying. The latter time made me wonder about the sex scene in NYC, so one day after work, the same week that the above betrayal occurred, I found a sex party where I could explore.

Spanking was always something I was attracted to, partially because so many men throughout my life had smacked my ass without consent. I had been spanked a few times by partners I had had consensually, although I had never been spanked as a child as punishment. There was pleasure in spanking for me to explore. I read the description and knew it was the party for me. It clearly stated that sex was not allowed and that full nudity was discouraged. I was excited to dip my toe in—to see if I even liked spanking as much as I had in the limited experiences I had already had.

Going to this event I was beyond nervous. I had already spent the money so I was locked in, but I remember pacing across the street from the venue. I repeated "If I want to leave I can leave at any time." My anxiety about doing something new was through the roof, but my drive to explore was greater. I made the conscious choice to explore.

The event started and I was one of two women present amongst seemingly nice but physically unattractive gentlemen who, although they were polite, looked at me like meat. I started a few conversations and tried to stay calm as people were arriving. I hadn't hit my social threshold or limit and sure enough a few more people arrived, I spotted a few I found attractive, and one older woman decided to take me under her wing. She showed me around the party and finally I knew I would stay. This woman was kind, she was guiding, and she was calming. I got to talking to a few couples. One couple in particular I was attracted to for a multitude of reasons.

The rest of the evening I spent speaking with this couple. I remember my first impressions of them very clearly. He caught my eye when they walked through the door to the event, as he reminded me, physically of a past lover of mine. She, however, was who caught my attention first and who I started talking to first. He was in the middle of us and I was sexually attracted to him but didn't quite know what to make of him. My natural distrust of men made me wary of him. I knew that I and she had a lot in common right away. I felt connected to her. There was a connection there that I gravitated toward but I was at a spank party; I was trying new things; I was saying yes. They were in a poly relationship and a Dominant Submissive relationship and this was intriguing to me; it invigorated my curiosity. I wanted to know more and see more, I wanted to experience them, but was scared to about what damage they could do to me, physically and mentally. I knew I was in a fragile place, but I was trying to heal.

Some of this world had been introduced to me but a lot of it was new and exciting. I felt empowered and exploring was also proving to be healing. We exchanged numbers and I remember texting him. I remember liking her and wanting to be her friend but I remember wanting him more. I remember there was something about her that was to similar to me, and that scared me. Contacting him felt easier than contacting her even though emotionally I felt more connected to her; I was looking for easy. Sex, for me, was easier. I was looking for fun. I was looking for the most basic levels of respect. Contacting him I remember I was nervous; I didn't know their rules. I didn't know what to expect. I remember feeling empowered and brave. He responded and gave me the lowdown that because they had met me together he could not pursue something separate with me. At the time I did not realize that this rule was placing my value at a lower level than the value of both of them. It was taking away choices I would then get to make in how I wanted this relationship to progress, and taking away respect from my contribution to the relationship in whatever form it would take. The relationship was now starting with disrespect but I didn't see this at the time, and it would be the biggest mistake.

The disappointment was swirling in my head, but I had never tried to date a couple and I remember clearly thinking: Why not try it? Maybe this will change my life. Maybe I like women more than I think I do. Exploring was definitely what was about to happen. We started off just exploring each other. I was and still am not sexually attracted to most women. The women I am attracted to are few and far between but I love kissing anyone and I am ok with others giving me pleasure. We discussed these boundaries and ideals and it started out being a safe space to be in, but soon that would change due to a lack of choices fueled by a lack of respect for me as an equal in this triad relationship.

There is a book out there, *More Than Two*, that is a great reference for poly couples or those exploring poly or anyone in any relationship and I can categorically state that by looking at a few passages in that book the three of us made a few big mistakes. I am going to try to stick to my own perceptions and observations as best I can because I truly believe everyone in the situation was doing the best they could with the choices given to them at the time. Presumptions vs. Assumptions are big battles however, because most people assume, when they should be presuming.

We had played together at least once all together and then we had the talk that resulted in me stating that I could not be sexual with the female part of the couple, that she could pleasure me but I would not reciprocate. It had nothing to do with beauty or attraction for her. I was very attracted to her as a person just not sexually. I can see though how me describing this so openly and honestly to her may have felt like a rejection. However, just like some people like chocolate and others don't, sexually speaking I did not want to pleasure her right then at that point, but I also didn't want to pleasure him at that point. It's interesting to look back on it now. Hindsight really can be eye opening.

It takes me a long time to want to touch someone else sexually. This is because of all the sexual abuse that until recently I didn't even realize was sexual abuse. My ability to understand people feeling pressured in sex is astronomical because I have ALWAYS, until my late twenties, felt pressured sexually—in all ways, by individuals and societally. **Everyone wants to be wanted though. In order for me to want to do anything sexually to another I have to know I want to; I have to trust them to tell me no if I cross a boundary.**

Having sex for me is fun and pleasurable but giving pleasure needs to have intention behind it; it needs to be consensual. The awareness that in sex I do not know what someone else wants is too present in the front of my mind when sex is involved because of my own experiences with abuse. It takes trust for me to want to touch someone sexually—trust in my own ability to know them, and their needs and wants. Not basic trust, but in-depth trust is essential for me to sexually want to please another person by making my own choices. My Mental Armor serves this purpose to know that sex can just be consensual casual sex, but it must remain respectful to not be considered rape. I start off wanting mutual pleasure yet me touching someone I don't know makes me insecure, afraid, panicked, worried, and physically ill. I know I cannot read someone's mind, so when I start out with someone, all I can tell them is what I like and dislike. Giving pleasure is something that takes time for me to want to do. Receiving pleasure is much easier for me in the beginning of a relationship so I can see if the other person is respectful to begin with and to then determine if they even respect themselves and truly are making conscious choices.

After I let them know my boundaries and capabilities I was friend zoned, which is ok. The three of us went on a date and now being friend zoned the energy changed in the group. We spent that day enjoying our outing but also discussing what was happening and it was a huge lesson in respect and the damage words can do. Humans say we don't like change, but choices are presented to us all the time; change happens as a result of those choices. Change is a part of life.

Let me explain: there are three distinct things I remember about our conversations. I remember being told that his priority will always be protecting her because she is his submissive, which I wanted because I didn't want to be viewed as a threat to their existing relationship. This automatically means I am always going to be second priority when I am with the two of them, and at this point we hadn't started spending time together separately. If I fucked this up I was losing two people—getting abandoned by two people. Which then led me to the choice of accepting this or walking away. I chose to continue until this choice became too negative for me to have to continue to make, I chose to respect their choices and take responsibility for my own. I was constantly being asked to choose between my own needs and the needs of the two of them.

The second thing I remember is wanting to listen to her in order to not be intentionally hurting a person I already cared about. At every turn this was difficult. When I asked how to make specific interactions easier there were no answers about needs or wants, and for someone who has never participated in this type of relationship this was very confusing and maddening. It made me question reality. If I don't know where the problem lies or what's needed to start to fix it, I can't take steps to do so, or adjust so the problem doesn't keep coming up. It became clear that I needed to protect myself because neither of them was doing it, and neither of them cared to actually listen to me or my needs. This was a relationship that possibly on its own is stable but having added me, now had created a separate seemingly unstable relationship. That was threatening my well-being.

There were always four relationships going on in my head when I entered the relationship their priority was as follows:

1. Theirs, just them.
2. Ours, all three of us.
   3A. Me and Her (Friendship; maybe sexual down the line).
   3B. Me and Him (Sexual; maybe friendship or more down the line).

The individual relationships needed to gain strength for my needs to be met. I needed to start dating separately because our relationship wasn't fulfilling my needs and in particular my desire to have sex with him. However, I also needed to start dating them separately because I felt so disrespected by constantly catering to her needs before my own. It all goes back to the start of the relationship and the choices being taken from me that were related to self respect. I was not aware of this at the time. My Mental Armor had some cracks in it.

Having never participated in a relationship like this, I needed to take baby steps and I couldn't imagine having sex with him in front of her as the first step. I was insecure as to the damage it may cause her, and I get lost in my brain already when it comes to sex because of past trauma and my abandonment fears. I knew what I needed. Yet my needs were hurtful to her.

The third thing I remember on that day was that I felt an expiration date was placed on the relationship as a whole. I knew this would not last long term. I knew they weren't treating me with respect and I could deal with it for now, but at some point this would get too hard and be to hurtful. At the time I couldn't place my exact feelings on it, but I knew that I would reach a breaking point where the negative effects of the relationship would outweigh the positives. I knew I would be at a depression low so great that all the things adding to it would boil over. At some point I would end up breaking up with them both. I hated this realization. I was in denial about it for a while because I knew it would be painful for not just me but both of them.

Before this relationship with these two people I had never tried this type of a relationship before but I remember feeling alone and abandoned on that day. There was good too though. Focusing on the good was healthy. I had never experienced a lot of the kink community and now I was getting to explore fantasies and wants I had always wanted to explore. I only continued because I knew I was capable of making choices as they were presented to me.

Here is a sexual realization I am not sure I would have come across if everything prior hadn't happened first:

Abandonment and My Sexual Submission

I had a parent die when I was little. The one that remained, although he did his best, was not entirely capable.

Parents, as society and nurturing standards dictate, are supposed to love, care, and protect you and to prepare you for autonomy. They are supposed to teach you and make sure you are not harmed physically, emotionally and mentally. They should give you the tools you need to exist in society and live a full life, including teaching you how to respect yourself first and then others. However, as you age, hurt and harm are inevitable and the gaps in your abilities to deal with reality shine through as a result of what knowledge you have gained prior.

The parent is supposed to then help you deal with the hurt and give you coping mechanisms or Mental Armor to carry on and realize it's all a part of our responsibility of living our own lives. They are supposed to help you understand your feelings and aid in you learning how to communicate needs and to help you exist in a world where good, amazing, bad, weird, and awful things happen.

**Parents are supposed to help you realize you are
the captain of your own ship and you can steer it
to any destination you choose. CHOICES.
Parents are there to help you understand your
choices, and how they will shape your life.**

I used "to suppose" "to" and "should" a lot and I
hate these words because reality is so much
different than expectation. Respect is so much more
complicated because of societal constructs. Being
capable is subjective and rarely is someone 100%
good at everything they do.

My parent that was left did their best. Thankfully
they re-married and that person, my step-parent,
raised me. Then through my own sheer will and
help from others along the way, I turned into a
pretty well-adjusted adult. Now, even healthy, I'd
say 95% of the time I give myself room to be kind
to my own humanity and to my ability to control my
own health at all times.

So what does this have to do with my submission?

I had one parent die and the other pretty incapable
(not their fault this parent was an orphan at sixteen
and did the best they could), but I was left feeling
abandoned by the people who chose to bring me
into this world. I felt unwanted and unsafe because
no one seemed to notice how much pain, suffering,
and harm was a part of my daily existence. I know
this unawareness is possible in others and sexually I

am submissive because I have respect for other's differences and challenges.

Now I crave to be wanted by someone who chooses me. I'm not looking for a mom or dad but someone who sees me as whole and who wants to be a support and a nourishing force and a partner in my life with mutual respect. This means reassuring me when I think he/she will leave me and telling me how wonderful he/she thinks I am and showing me not just with words but actions that I matter in their life—that I am a priority. I'm not sure I have ever felt like a priority to my family, but especially my parents. **I am not sure I have ever felt like a priority to anyone in my entire life other than to myself.**

I need someone who is whole themselves because I do not need to fix anyone; I've done enough fixing of myself. I also truly know that if you don't want to change, you won't.

Sexually speaking, I am looking for someone confident and keen on telling me what to do and who has morals and needs that match my own. I over-think everything because I've experienced loss and tragedy and hurt and happiness and disappointment and love and so many things that I was prepared and unprepared to handle. By thinking about all possibilities it calms and excites me and can sometimes overwhelm and bring me anxiety. It is so entirely who I am, and helps me experience life with an open mind to know I have thought about all outcomes so that I feel prepared.

I don't want to think that much for sex. I want to just enjoy the pleasure of sex. When I do over-think it's hard to orgasm and hard to enjoy myself. When it come to sex, I like to let someone else take control, be in charge, make decisions, and tell me what to do because then, even though I maintain control of myself and my consent, my partner is pleased and it's one less worry I have that I will disappoint. It is one less responsibility to take on that is not mine to take on—one less thought that I will let the other person, and ultimately myself, down. One less worry about disrespecting someone even if it is myself. If I have a person that is confident and knows what they want and can clearly communicate and be honest, it gives me confidence that we can tackle anything and that I can be what they need and they can be what I need—and that is to enrich and go through life together with respect and hopefully love.

Growing up I had little of the above in the sense of consistency or good emotional health or parents that knew how to handle my mental illness. I was a third child and often got hand-me-downs and no boundaries and wasn't disciplined and had to learn as an adult what respect meant.

I was privileged in the sense that I had a roof over my head and clothes and food. I went to school and college and I know I was better off than some. I had more choices than many. However, I felt neglected in a lot of ways. My abuse was massive. I don't remember a sense of safety, and I also didn't know if someone had asked if I felt safe whether I would have been able to say yes. I didn't know I had a right to feel safe. I didn't know safety was important to living.

Now all I want is to be respected at all times and try to give others the most respect I can without violating my own needs and being worried that if I violate their boundaries they will leave. If they leave then they don't understand respect or haven't seen themselves clearly—or maybe I am too triggering for them. I have a say in who I have relationships with. I have a say in who disrespects me and who I allow to hurt me, because I am aware of my mental capabilities to make choices. My Mental Armor is growing and changing and strengthening.

As a friend pointed out, I always have the choice to leave as well, but as someone who has been abandoned over and over by everyone in my life, I have tended to stick my claws in and not let go of people I truly care about because I felt overly responsible to make sure they did not feel abandoned by me. However, other people's feelings are not my responsibility when it comes to disrespecting my own needs.

My trauma and abandonment is so present from my childhood; it feeds every negative thought I have. I

have done so much work to relinquish the chains
that I feel shackled with by my abandonment and I
sometimes worry they will never truly be lifted off
my brain. This is why I am strengthening my mind,
but allowing for the submissive tendencies to add to
that strength.

■■

Writing the above I remember feeling lighter, like
my sexual submission was always something I
knew. It was my way of finally getting the safety
and caring attention I was lacking when growing up
but applying it to my sexual self.

Sex between two people can be complicated
but sex between three, from my experience, is
greatly more complicated when insecurities are
present. I dated the couple I mentioned above until
October 2019. Breaking up with them took a lot of
courage and was really hard.

While I had been dating the couple I met a
man online through a sex positive social media sight
geared toward fetishes and kink, and an
empowering respectful sexual environment for
expression, called Fetlife. I fell in love with him. At
the time I was in denial about how much I cared for
him but he was in process of abandoning me. I was
in the process of trying to do better at work, which
was abusive and causing me suicidal thoughts. I felt
entirely unsupported and trapped in my relationship
with this couple which was not helping the
situation.

Every time I would hang out separately with the man the woman could not handle it. I would receive horrid texts from her and I would allow her to vent and feel her feelings but at times they felt quit mean, hurtful, and truly damaging to me. I felt like a beaten dog. I was being mentally and verbally abused at work and by this woman who at the time I cared for immensely and loved, and the negatives started to outweigh the positives. I was constantly being told by her that I was a threat to her relationship. Whether she realized she was saying that or not, she implied it over, and over, and over again.

When I met with the man in the park to break up with them, it wasn't ideal. Breaking up with one person through text was hard but with two, I felt like a coward. Nonetheless, I was feeling worthless and suicidal and needed to do something to alleviate the stress that was not intentionally harmful. I had agreed to it because I felt obligated and while I was speaking to him I realized some troubling facts about my feelings toward the woman. I had held back information about my ex— the man I was in love with while on cruise ships— and it was because the woman reminded me of him. She was unable at time to express her needs or wants, and she was working so hard on herself but she so vividly reminded me of him. She reminded me of myself as well, at different times in my life when I was not seeing things clearly and my flight or fight responses were kicking in. She triggered me constantly, and felt abusive and like I was allowing her to manipulate me constantly. Looking back I know without a doubt she was not doing this on purpose, or I hope she wasn't, which is why when I realized I needed out for me, I broke up with them both.

At one point in my life I never thought I would turn down love—turn down someone who wanted to be close to me—but both my ex and this woman whom I loved and cared for were, in my opinion, barely capable of getting through each day, and I am not their hero. I couldn't be her hero because I was trying to be my own. She and my ex never asked me to be their hero, so I needed to end those relationships out of respect for us both. With the man I was in love with I was willing to compromise myself for him because I was in love with him but for this woman, I was not in love with her, and had to choose myself. It was the only way to respect her needs and my own.

I did not want to constantly be defending myself or my needs to someone—anyone. I wanted to feel respected and able to respect her needs, my needs, and the man's needs. I felt trapped and ended it with both of them. It was one of the hardest things to do because I knew she was going to feel abandoned by me but I wanted to stop feeling like I was hurting her. Once I realized I was never going to feel like I was not hurting her in that specific triad relationship, I made the decision to end it. I wanted to not feel trapped without a way to do what was right for me.

A few months went by and he contacted me, very casually. When I ended things with both of them he had asked if he could contact me, and I said yes. I asked if the woman knew and had consented to him contacting me and he said she had. It was casual, at first. A text here—a text there. I didn't instigate the texting, and it was cordial. There wasn't a ton of meaning for me, and I didn't mind it. Then he asked to see me.

The nerves I had walking into that apartment were drastic. I thought I would never see it again and so it was surreal. It was slightly triggering but I looked at it positively. Yet being around him was quite easy. That was what I wanted. Ease. I needed this to be a purely sexual relationship when I started seeing this man because sex was the only way in the triad relationship I ever felt respected by either of them. I couldn't worry that I would fall in love with him; I couldn't worry what the woman would think. I needed easy. I was also being respectful to him when he reached out to me and showed me that he listened to me. I didn't know until later we would have to go through all the ways he disrespected me in the first place to have a healthy relationship.

Figuring out how this was going to work was new territory. I had never started a sexual relationship with a lateral polyamorous man. I didn't know how it might change me, or the realizations it would provide. I was scared but curious. This was what I wanted when I first reached out—to get to know him and get to know what his intentions were. Up until now I thought he only ever wanted me for sex, so I was ready to enjoy sex with him but to also see what else could be. I didn't have any emotions involved because my expectations were about respect. I didn't think he was emotionally capable of giving me more than sex, because he had emotionally been a part of the abuse I had in the previous relationship. He had added to me being secluded. He had shown me as much disrespect as she had. What's worse is he didn't realize it. What I didn't realize is his level of respect was great; he was cautious in the same ways I was, and respectful in the same ways as well. This was confusing because I knew at some point the woman would come back up. I was curious to see how. If it was easy and reflective maybe she was ready; maybe I was wrong. Maybe she wasn't like my ex. Unfortunately, she was.

"Mental illness makes life a choice"

19. Clarity

When you go from being someone who never thought you would find love, to being madly in love, to trying not to be entirely discouraged by life because dating is awful and abandonment is everywhere, it is hard to not think of the worst case scenarios even when you are having amazing sex.

One of those worst case scenarios was the fear I had that the woman from the couple would

present an ultimatum to the man that if he kept
sleeping with me that she would break up with him.
That happened about four weeks ago. Which was
interesting for me. It was hard for me.

It also was not supposed to be an ultimatum
even though I presumptively thought it was. Instead
it was an expression of her feelings that she does
not know if she can get over her own hurt that was
caused by my actions. However, she does not see
how my actions were originally influenced by the
restrictions of my choices, and the disrespectful
nature that we started the triad relationship in the
first place.

I met up with the man and he told me that
the woman had told him that she may break up with
him if he continues seeing me. My initial reaction
was, "Ok, how do I process this? What does he
want me to say? What is he thinking? Why is he
telling me this? What does he want? Does this mean
he's breaking things off with me? Why do I feel
trapped again?"

After our conversation I had to break down
my emotions. I figured out that I was disappointed
because I broke up with them both the first time
because I didn't want this exact thing. I needed easy
and this conversation was not easy; it was
uncomfortable and upsetting for a lot of reasons. I
felt like the villain of her story. This is the exact
opposite of where I wanted to be so why didn't I

break up with him again? Why did I allow our relationship to not be phased by this ultimatum?

When I asked why he was telling me, he stated he wanted me to have the information. I asked then what were his expectations from me? He didn't have any and so I told him how this made me feel really uncomfortable because if she's going to make that choice then she is going to make that choice. I feel bad for him because she put him in that position but I'm also not surprised and had already prepared for this conversation on my own a few times. I was angry because I felt he was disrespected. My anger had to do with her disrespect for him, and my protective nature of him giving me this perception. She is entitled to be angry with me; I hurt her. However, until she sees how she disrespected me from the start of the triad relationship, she will never be able to understand why I made the choices I made. He however is also entitled to pursue his own relationship with me, so my choice was simple: Do I want to keep seeing him?

Up until this point I knew who he was but this conversation was where he proved to me that what I thought was right. He is the poly man who has lateral relationships; each one is separate and he wants to be able to sleep with whomever he wants. He believes in respecting his partners by first respecting himself. The woman was telling him that if he keeps seeing me then she might break up with him, and that's disrespectful to him because she doesn't get to make that choice for him—only for herself. I felt really bad for him because it really could have been anyone in my shoes but it wasn't; it was me, so I also felt proud. I ended the conversation by making sure he knew that I was cool with us keeping seeing each other and that I respect his decision either way. This relationship is me and him and I don't take the woman's needs into account out of my immense respect for our relationship. The truth is I would rather him choose her. I would rather him dump me, but making that choice for him would be disrespectful to myself and to him. I no longer felt any allegiance to her because she had shown me so much disrespect that she felt dangerous to my ability to live.

However, there were some negative effects with this interaction. It made me trust the man less with emotional information I give him that may hurt the woman. I worried that he doesn't understand the proper questions to ask her when she disrespects him, and I worried how our relationship may be negatively affected if this kind of issue comes up again. I walked away from that conversation truly hoping three things: 1) I hope she doesn't break up with him because of me. 2) I hope they get past this. 3) I have love for the guy that I need to express but this incident makes it really hard to keep things easy and I lost a little perceived trust with him. The only way for me to get the trust back is telling him everything I have kept from him and allow him the respect to have all the information. Show him my love—not just tell him. However, I cannot expose myself to him like this until I know I am in love with him.

On a side note: I don't know if she would ever break it off with him but that's not my business to talk about. However, this whole thing has put a fracture in my trust with him because now I am afraid to tell him that I have a care and love for him. I was afraid to tell him my feelings had changed. He had moved from the category of "just sex" to having more potential. Once I worked through these feelings, I was able to express myself.

This relationship with this man has been different than any other relationship. **The ups and downs in the beginning were rough**. Now that it is me and him and him and others, in a more lateral way, it's become simpler. I just want to open up to him and tell him the changes.

When you are sitting on your bed talking to yourself about how to tell a man that you love him in a cordial way, it feels nice to be confident in doing it. There is still that whisper in the back of my mind that this could be the one thing that makes him leave. This could be the reason he decides he doesn't want to talk to me; this could be why he leaves, is a sobering reality. It's also sobering because it could be the thing that makes me leave him. Love is absolutely something worth living and dying for, and I talk about how I learned this through a movie.

I'm about to turn thirty and my best friend wrote on my mirror that "Psss… your anxiety is lying to you." She is beyond right in one way, and every time I start to feel anxious about anything I look at that and it helps remind me. However, until I understood where my anxiety stemmed from and how to snap my brain back to reality, and breathe through it, it was really, really difficult for me to grasp this concept. I have a choice to listen to the anxiety and let it affect me or I can choose to try and understand the anxiety and face it—to deal with it and to try to make choices to lessen it. My anxiety stems from fear of abandonment at every turn, even by myself. There have been times in my life I felt I abandoned myself, where I made the wrong choice, and I am so grateful that I never made the wrong choice when it came to living.

However, there are those out there that don't see life as a choice, they see it as a right. ***Mental illness and mental health makes life a choice, and Mental Armor helps us fight the illness.*** I disagree usually with the people that think life is a right because of religion. I look at it from my agnostic perspective; I do not believe there is a god, and I also believe god could exist. The only thing I can count on is that when a choice presents itself to me, I make the best decision in that moment to further my life toward my goals. For the longest time, my goal was to learn about myself. The want to not feel so abandoned was driving my self awareness, and finally I found the last puzzle piece to make it, so I show up and never feel abandoned by myself. This doesn't mean I don't make mistakes, but I can own my mistakes and admit them to myself and others and this is only because I know without a doubt I will always be on my side, and I will always look after my mental health first because my Mental Armor is so much stronger than I ever knew.

"I started rebuilding and exploring sex as a way to free myself from the hurt of perceived humanity"

20. Puzzle Complete. On to the next.

Describing my life in the way I see it has always been hard because life is unpredictable. Reality is individual. With the knowledge I have now, and hopefully with each new learning experience, I will continue to work on my life puzzles. Puzzles are always something I enjoyed doing with my middle sister and I am immensely happy we did them together; it showed me how important help is in life. However, these metaphorical puzzles that are my way of looking at life can be complete and then out of nowhere a new puzzle piece can be found. Puzzles also can be restored.

My mind is my puzzle and always has been. For the longest time I was trying to solve the puzzle so I could see the whole picture—zoom in on the pieces and learn or find new puzzle pieces I felt were missing or couldn't figure out where they fit. People often describe missing puzzle pieces as holes they feel, in terms of love, or limitations in life, or any number of descriptions to illustrate goals. My limitations or lack of knowledge, or goals unfulfilled never felt like a hole because I was always grateful for the pieces I had found. When I was able to be in the present, I thought I knew myself—my drives, my brain. When I would evaluate who I was, I never cowered at the fear of learning new and exciting things about myself because learning is amazing. It wasn't until I found the last piece of my mind puzzle that I was able to zoom out and see the bigger picture, to see what was truly important to me and what I wanted my full puzzle to represent. I was always driven to explore my motivation, desires, capabilities, boundaries, intellect, relationships, and life, just like so many others are also hunting for purpose.

On March 21, 2020 as Corona Virus was coming into prominence I wrote this journal entry:

<u>Timeline...</u>

My mother died when I was five. Two years later my dad married my step-mom. When I was eight, my breasts started to grow. I was ten when I got my first peck on my cheek and realized I liked a boy next door. I started masturbating at ten and watching porn at ten. I was eleven when 9/11 happened. Eleven was also the year I was first touched inappropriately while at sleep away camp. At thirteen I had my first kiss, and also felt forced to allow him to touch my breasts. I remember wanting to say no, but wanting my first kiss more. I started taking photos of myself before selfies were a thing. At fourteen I knew I could get attention for my boobs. At fifteen I got called a butter face. At sixteen I understood I could put a man in jail for sex, but didn't understand why they didn't have the same understanding about touching others inappropriately. By sixteen I felt utterly disgusted by my body. Now, when I look back, I am so happy I took those pictures because I was not kind to myself. I was beautiful; I just couldn't see it. I turned seventeen and I got to drive. Between sixteen and seventeen is also the year my aunt almost succeeded with committing suicide and my step-mom was hit as a pedestrian by a drunk driver. Seventeen is the year I got my breast reduction. Finally, at eighteen, I graduated high school and made it to college. I was finally out of my parents' abusive house. They did their best but I was abused verbally and mentally, unintentionally. I love my parents, and they did keep me alive; they just also didn't see how much self harm I was doing to myself. However, eighteen brought on a lot of sexual firsts as well. My first relationship at a job, first blow job, the first time I should have followed my gut with a man. At nineteen I lost my virginity to my predatory boss. I didn't realize it at the time but it was a Dom/Sub relationship, but he was my boss, and I could have gotten him in trouble. He didn't pressure me, but he also didn't respect me. Consent was never taught to me in terms of feeling like I had a right to my body because I don't know if anyone said it in a way I would have been able to hear because of my mother's disrespect to her own body by committing suicide. Society and government are also largely unaware at the message they send to women: that our bodies are not our own. My boss never found out he was my first. I doubt I'll ever tell him. However, I did love him, and that was when I got diagnosed with anxiety and panic attacks. Twenty was when I got my first job that was so very important to me and I fell in love with a man that could not love me back. Twenty-one was when I made my first friend that will hopefully stay my friend forever. At twenty-two, I graduated college which was no easy task. At twenty-three, I lived in D.C. Twenty-four I worked for Broadway and fell in love with a man who had the courage to love me back but not love himself. Twenty-five my world felt broken, but I pieced it back together. Twenty-six I went out on my own. Twenty-seven I started an adventure. Twenty-eight I basked in the glory of all my experiences and got shattered by the greed and fear that lead other humans to discriminate against me and leave me utterly broken. Twenty-eight was also the year I was broken by a corporation. **Twenty-nine I started rebuilding and exploring sex as a way to free myself from the hurt of perceived humanity**. Age thirty is when I found my true self and realized I am the superhero I always wanted to be and my choices are so much more powerful than I ever knew. The world might be falling apart right now but I want to remember my strength in this time of sorrow and grief. I am in mourning for the world that was just murdered by virus. I feel responsible because I am a human and know my responsibility. Responsibility was instilled in me the moment my mother took her own life and I felt responsible. However, through all of my struggles I remember that I have people I love and can help me to live, by

just living, and making the choice to live. You have
the power to make that choice even if you are not
privileged with love like I am. You and you alone.
Be kind to your fellow human, and see that they are
more than their body, more than their sexual
appetite, more than a means to an end, more than
the single puzzle piece you might be trying to place
in your own puzzle. Be kind not because you hope
they will be kind to you, but because it feels good to
know you made their day better, and not worse—to
know that you were not an inconvenience or caused
them pain, and maybe that will feel like a way to
much joy to fill your body... and then guess what,
go be nice and kind to someone else or work on
being kind to yourself. If all else fails, use your wit,
intelligence, and humor to fight fear with kindness.
To fight fear with logic. To fight fear with your
Mental Armor. Pick and choose those battles
though, for sometimes walking away is the truly
only kind thing you can do for another human. This
other human may be the choice of saving yourself
from the harm they can do to you. Remember, your
choices matter. A concept that I try to go by from
the movie *The Hate U Give*, I live for the things I'd
die for, and I'd die for the things that help me live.
Help one another, and try your hardest to not hurt...
unless you like a little pain with your pleasure. ;)

Our world once again shifted in 2020, and not in a
small way. I have had so much experience with
trauma and change that I crave it at times because it
has provided for the biggest amount of learning in
my life. I found myself quickly experiencing new

trauma with a quicker response; it was like I had new experiences that were being supported by my previous experiences, so that I could adapt quicker. My foundation is strong and it helped me to keep building my mental strength—my Mental Armor. Building my Mental Armor and knowing I don't have one type of armor is freeing.

Every single step I took to better myself was finding a new puzzle piece and adding it to my puzzle. Now that one puzzle is complete I can zoom in on each piece and see the imperfections or scratches and each time I get more information it's like being able to zoom around and see the individual pixels making the puzzle. I can see the tiniest scratch and verbalize insecurities or fears or love with no worry or fear that it will break my puzzle apart because I have taken super glue and framed the thing on my wall in my mind. No one can break my puzzle.

Growing up as I have described I took care of myself. Even when others tried to take care of me, I in part, wasn't capable of letting them or even seeing that they were trying. My imposter syndrome always kicked in and said "YOU DON'T KNOW ME." Only I know me. My step-mom did more for me than I knew; she wasn't perfect but she did the best she could to show me she loved me and wasn't going anywhere. She saved my life. That doesn't mean I felt safe and it doesn't mean I don't have trauma inflicted by her actions; it doesn't dissipate her lack of capabilities to be the parent I needed.

The mother I lost to mental illness will always influence my fear, my anxiety, my worry, and my love. **What it means is that both of my moms were and are a part of my puzzle and they helped me to gather pieces I needed to not follow in the footsteps of all the people I have admired in life, and choose my own path.** That's how I feel about every person in my life now. They each, uniquely, influenced my life in ways, positive and negative, to help me get my next puzzle piece. As a happy and healthy adult, I feel incredibly grateful for all my experiences with every person.

Everyone is going through life the best they can; they are doing the best they can with the information they have first and foremost about themselves, and their needs. Life is a giant experiment, and the ultimate part of the experiment is making the choices in front of us that keep us and others alive. In my opinion we are all selfishly motivated—even those that are religious. The commonality of our ability to choose has become extremely enlightening and speaks to my value of respecting yourself and others in the best way possible with the information you have. I am not religious with the exception of the cultural aspects that I hold dear. I think I am quite spiritual. I believe in the universe. I love stories. I love speaking about stories and my own experiences and actively listening to others so I can connect to the commonality between me and other humans. I live for experiences and learning and changing. I live for bringing kindness and joy and happiness to others and helping others who will allow me to be there for them or ask me for help. This is shown in the respect I have for others. Creativity and producing is also how I live.

Boundaries and our limits of negative behavior can be hard to understand and truly see at times. If we do not know ourselves first and our true motivations, or why certain actions or choices trigger negative emotions, then how can we work to lesson our emotional reactions when they happen? How do we use logic over emotion?

Until you have complete or a large amount of self awareness or are willing to admit the information to yourself, it's hard to overcome the negative feelings and past triggers from trauma. This is 100% the case for me because it's how I live my life and how I have observed others living their lives. I have always been trying to better my mind puzzle and now I can start working on other puzzles that I value.

As an example, I am currently working on my sexual puzzle which I am currently exploring and learning. I am constantly bettering my respect puzzle in relation to my own image and trying to overcome my self-diagnosed imposter syndrome. I am always working on my family puzzle. I am always working on my relationships puzzle. I am always working on my learning puzzle. I am always working on my communication puzzle. I am always working on my strength puzzle, both physically and mentally.

The puzzle that is just starting to form is how can I help others feel this amazing about themselves? How do I get the message out there that whether it's religion or family or yourself, whatever path you take to build your puzzle and create your story, **live your life how you choose to live it**. It is important that you try every day until you feel like the picture is as complete as it can be. It is also important that you realize you are a part of every other person's life puzzle that you come across. It is your choice as to what type of puzzle piece you allow the other person to create. There are plenty of times in my life that I was proud of who I was. I look back and have absolutely no regrets or modifications I would make because they all lead to now. It's in a way a religious experience, because it feels as though the people you hear of having this same self-assured awareness often talk about the feeling I have in terms of finding god. However, I talk about it in respect to the view and knowledge we gain about our own lives and it has nothing to do with god and everything to do with humanity.

I am thankful every day that I have a complete mind puzzle and now I will work very hard each day to maintain that puzzle and make sure no one and nothing see my big picture differently than the way I see it. You may think that sounds selfish. If I were talking about faith in god, would you think the same? Self pride and working on ourselves is part of the change I think this world needs. We do not spend enough time on mental illness, or sex, or abuse, or love, or any complex emotion, ideology, or word. We have a CHOICE. These are topics and concepts that make our minds think, which is why I am going back to school to try to professionally help others think and grow, if they want to have my help.

As I wrote this book the mention of mental illness was hard, because people stigmatize it. I wanted a way to talk about mental illness while being positive about my experiences with it. That's why I created my own ideologies, like Kindism, Respectism, Happism, and choose to battle my mental illness with my Mental Armor. Some may call my coping mechanisms wrong or inadequate or shameful. I call them my shield, my indication that someone has wronged me the way I see me, and that I need to be my own hero and stand up for myself. I do not need to be laying my life down for others who disrespect me unless they are incapable of saving themselves. If I am going to use my powers for good then I need to get certified to do so, because I know others may and always have called me a know it all. They didn't see me for my experiences.

To really drive this home: here is a writing I have from before I stared journaling at nineteen. It was the first time I can remember referencing puzzle pieces and it truly speaks to my entire philosophy and shows how lost I once was, yet still

knowing what questions I needed to find answers
to:

How do you tell people they are not a part of your
life? How do you tell them they never really knew
you? How do you say, "I know your secrets but you
can't know mine"? At what point do you let
someone into your head? How much of me should I
let the people around me see? Can they handle it?
Can I handle it? What if they desert me? She
deserted me. And she was of blood. If someone
that's supposed to love you can do such a thing,
then what stops the rest? I can't lose another. I
won't. So I push them away, far away. You don't
know me. How can you? I only let out pieces of me
so that no one can complete the puzzle. That's what
I am; I'm a puzzle. Only I wish pieces weren't
missing. I wish I could let them see—see the real
me. There are just too many pieces, and some have
already been bent and damaged. My heart aches, for
I know who I am but no one else shall see. I am a
puzzle and it is true; I am too complicated for YOU.
▪▪

If I hadn't had theater, or my experiences in work,
or any number of experiences I covered in this
book, I don't know if I would have found myself
and my purpose.

My respect for life has been growing since I
was five and showed blatantly how disrespectful
others are about human life, including sometimes
their own life. I realized I wanted to help others and
my drive was always about my need to help and not

harm. To be a reason people wouldn't be hurt is what my mother taught me, and yet it took me many years to determine I was a person too that did not have to follow in my mother's footsteps.

Keep going; keep building; keep making the choice to live. There is never such a thing as too old or too young to work on figuring out how your own mind works and what will bring you happiness and complete that puzzle. Your armor or shield or abilities or education can help you to understand this universe. **<u>Death, although scary, makes me respect my life</u>**, because death is inevitable. Death is what brings value to life. No one truly knows what kind of adventure that is, so in the meantime I am going to have the best adventure I can with life. I will listen to my body and mind and show it the respect of life before death. All I can do is make a choice with the options I have in front of me, and be prepared for those that will come my way. I can hope that I can apologize for the mistakes I have made and will make.

As I wrap this memoir up, I admit that the times we are entering feel uncertain. CoVid-19 is in full swing. It is April 22, 2020, and our economy is crashing, our former way of life has utterly been wiped away, and yet people continue to show that they do not care about their fellow humans' lives. Others, and thankfully we are in the majority, choose to get past their fear and help each other in times of life or death. For someone who feels responsible for the world, this is hard. For healthcare workers this is unimaginable. I am lately in the middle of trying to go back to school to get my social work graduate degree. Helping those with mental illness and help in the wake of this world pandemic, but always helping others, has been my goal. This virus is exposing the world and specifically my home country as the broken global emergency that so many feared it would become.

My Mental Armor is most important in this time, when I hope and in some ways spread my prayers that people will see the truth. See how broken our government is in the USA, and choose someone with integrity, someone who is honest, and someone who fights for humans to lead our country out of the darkness that it feels we are plummeting toward. I wish humans were not thought of as money. However, in a capitalist society I am painfully aware that they are considered dollars.

If my logic is correct then we, as the US, are the second richest country in the world. China, a communist country is the only one currently that has more humans than us. If money = humans, then Social Democracy is not the same as socialism, and not the same as communism. It is in my opinion the only safe government. It allows for social changes to affect our government and leaders in a moral and ethical way when racism and negative respect values exist in far too many people. Trump unfortunately has only ever cared about money. In the face of a pandemic I hope he realized that without people who support him, he will be left with nothing, and probably in jail. **<u>A virus does not choose who it kills. Only humans have this choice between life or death or living.</u>**

I never thought I would become a humanitarian activist but wanting to help others create Mental Armor to protect their mental wounds has now become more important than ever. Our world, and the country where I was born, feels like Nazi Germany right now. People by the hundreds and thousands are expendable to the government because of money. Yet money seems like an ever-flowing waterfall to those in power. How do you overlook the message you are sending so many people that their lives don't matter? How do you blatantly not understand the message of disrespect you send to the people you govern when you do not handle a global pandemic with proper attention and leadership? Millions of lives are in danger. **<u>Responsibility falls on those in leadership roles.</u>**

The other day I realized that I was at one-point part of the problem. Five years ago before the last election, I didn't want to see the corruption. I didn't want to see that companies valued money over human life. I didn't want to see that people would murder for money. I was naïve to the evils that people commit in the name of all sorts of things, whether it be god, or duty, or life. Perception is powerful. Assumptions are powerful and presumptions are powerful if you don't realize you are treating them as assumptions. I have become very grateful that my perception is based in reality;

it is based in the science of my mind, body, and the universe. To be a Kindist, Respectist, and Happist is what I believe it is to be born in the United States, and I am proud to be from this country, even if there is embarrassment currently to be from the USA. We have always been a country that says it can be better. Maybe this act of Mother Nature, or as religious people might say, act of god, can point us in the direction of how to be kinder to people. To respect people. To allow all people to pursue happiness.

Becoming an activist was never a goal of mine. Twitter arguments were never something I thought I would regularly partake in or even enjoy. Discord is extremely enlightening. However, when I started realizing how much I valued others' opinions and how much I trusted my own it was hard to not become an activist for humans—for respecting humans. The responsibility was overwhelming.

Mental armor can be faith or religion; it can be education and self awareness in order to fight off the mental illness that has, at times told me to disrespect my own life. At time mental illness has told me to disrespect others. Mental armor is the tool we can use to fight off any threat to ourselves, whether physical or mental. Mental armor is a choice we can make to not knowingly harm others and respect all humans.

Mental Armor is Consciousness and Cognitive Strength

Respecting myself is about looking at all the choices, and seeing which is right for me. A person's right to choice is the most important respect we can show ourselves and others. It is for some the last piece of their self-respect puzzle that allows them to truly respect others. It is imperative to realize your own place in your life before you start taking an active role in other people's lives. We individually have more power than we think, because as we band together we create more commonality. We create a collective. We help one another so that we may help ourselves. We use our alone nature to be together in protecting one another. You cannot deny we enter this world alone and unique, and each of us dies alone having lived a unique life that we chose, hopefully with others.

We go through life experiencing it. That is what life is about. Mental Armor is a tool. It is a way to experience everything life has to offer without the worry or fear of the negative effects. Life may have caused you trauma in the past, and it still might in the future. Armor does not need to be rigid. It can be made of whatever materials you have on hand or can imagine in your mind. Protecting the mind, which makes up the person you choose to be, is of the upmost importance in keeping you living. We often hear about people having walls built up to protect them. Walls are structures; once built they are hard to tear down; they leave materials when they come down and they are confining. Armor can be breathable. It protects and can be voluntarily discarded once the wearer feels safe. Armor allows for movement and flexibility if you so choose. It is a tool used to help its owner feel safe in any situation that may come along in life. However, it also makes you aware that others may try and breach your Mental Armor.

Choosing a path, no matter your background or your beliefs, is a responsibility each human has as a cognitive being.

<u>My contribution will always be: Let your Mental Armor glisten, for we all have that armor to protect ourselves against our own demise or the demise others may or can inflict.</u>

This armor makes us stronger, and helps us to respect the life we choose to live each day. Mental Armor is there to help us defeat and keep our mental illness from winning—from taking our brains hostage—and it allows us to fight every second of every day. Stay strong. Fight for your Mental Armor; fight for the choices that are humanly your right to make and choose without possibly causing harm to others. Above all else, respect your life; try to love and respect yourself and know you are not alone if you allow others to be alone with you. Relationships are just a choice to enjoy someone's company and live together.

My Jewish culture is very important to me; it taught me how important family is and it taught me how important questions are to life and living. I have had a few people in my life that have made me feel comfortable about asking them questions without anxiety that they may be offended.

Asking people questions is to me like looking through someone's phone without permission. Getting more confident in asking question was a skill I needed to learn and at this point I believe I have improved, still a work in progress.

Growing up, Passover was always my favorite holiday because it told a story about my Jewish heritage. In that story the children ask questions and they are described as wise, wicked, simple, and unknowing. These questions and the story telling of god shaped my life more than I knew. Passover saved my life. Religion, even though I am now agnostic and do not believe in god or that god does not exist, is huge in me never taking my own life. I would implore you, if you have made this far to think about the following questions:

How do you build Mental Armor?
How do you become more conscious of the choices you are making for yourself and in partnerships or relationships with other adults in a mutually respectful way for all humans involved?

By asking questions first and making presumptions or observations, not assumptions, you are giving yourself respect and others respect. By giving humans the benefit of the doubt that they, just like you, are doing their best to live each day by choosing life over death, you could be saving a life. It is not your responsibility once you are an adult to determine the reasoning or take on the responsibility of other people's choices. You are only responsible for your choices. **<u>Respect yourself first, use your Mental Armor to accomplish this, and then make choices that show yourself that you deserve to live because you are in fact alive.</u>**

    GLOBAL RESPECT, REFORM, and EDUCATION on RESPECT are NEEDED.